Featherstone

CREATIVE PLANNING IN THE EYFS

Autumn

Lucy Peet

 Linked closely to the revised Early Years Foundation Stage (2012)

 Six weeks of differentiated planning

 Coverage across the 7 areas and 17 aspects of learning

 Activities based upon Playing and Exploring, Active Learning, Creating and Thinking Critically

Guidance on assessing characterisitics of learning

Published 2012 by Featherstone Education
Bloomsbury Publishing Plc
50 Bedford Square, London, WC1B 3DP
www.bloomsbury.com

ISBN 978-1-4081-7-3923

Text © Lucy Peet 2012
Design © Lynda Murray
Photographs © Shutterstock

Printed in Great Britain by Latimer Trend & Company Ltd

10 9 8 7 6 5 4 3 2 1

This book is produced using paper that is made from wood grown in
managed, sustainable forests. It is natural, renewable and recyclable.
The logging and manufacturing processes conform to the environmental
regulations of the country of origin.

To see our full range of titles visit www.bloomsbury.com

Contents

Introduction

About the series

This book is part of a series written for all who work with children in the Foundation Stage (FS). Owing to the fun, practical nature of the activities it is suitable for a wide range of settings, including schools, pre-schools, childminders and nurseries. Given that all the activities are differentiated for children working towards the Early Learning Goals (ELGs) 'the knowledge, skills and understanding children should have at the end of the academic year in which they turn five' (p.2, 2012), it is particularly relevant to practitioners working with FS1, FS2 and mixed-age classes. However, with the increasing good practice of the FS extending into Year 1 and 2 this book is invaluable for teachers wishing to promote active learning and a creative curriculum with children up to the age of seven. Each activity links with the requirements and expectations of the National Curriculum, statutory for Key Stage 1 in England and Wales, and through observation it will also be possible to collect evidence for Assessing Pupils' Progress. The table below shows the corresponding year groups for children from Scotland and Northern Ireland.

Year groups and corresponding ages:

Age	School year		
	England and Wales	**Scotland**	**Northern Ireland**
2 - 3	Foundation Stage		
3 - 4	FS1 (previously nursery)		P 1
4 - 5	FS2 (previously reception)	Primary 1	P 2
5 - 6	Year 1	Primary 2	P 3
6 - 7	Year 2	Primary 3	P 4

How this book is structured

Through the topic of autumn children will be involved in playing and exploring, active learning and creating and thinking critically: all key features of the revised Early Years Foundation Stage (EYFS) (2012). This book contains six weeks of planning – five weeks of detailed plans, with an activity designed for each specific area of learning, and a celebratory week of activity to share with parents and carers at the end covering the 'prime areas of learning'. Details are shown in the six week planning overview grid on page 62.

Activities are structured to build upon children's skills over the six weeks developing their experiences and abilities. For example, week 1 introduces a literacy activity where the children go on a walk, using their senses to describe what they can see. This skill is extended in week 4 when they can use some of the same vocabulary to describe natural autumnal objects to their partner, focusing on listening and questioning in pairs. Colour mixing in week 3 is extended in week 4, where pattern is introduced to complement the shade and tone work already undertaken. The 3D shape work in week 3 is consolidated in week 5, when the children use box modelling to create rockets and fireworks.

Through this method of extending similar tasks at a later date children are able to consolidate their knowledge and practise their skills. The final week of celebration is an opportunity to share the topic with parents and carers.

Each activity is clearly structured, with suggestions for:

◆ Resources required with relevant storybook or non-fiction book suggestions to support the main idea

◆ Key vocabulary

◆ A simple 'what to do' explanation with ideas for both guided and independent activity

◆ Differentiation of the activity at three levels. Each activity is pitched at an average level of understanding in line with the expected level of the ELGs. There are also ideas to **support** children who are working at the emerging stage and to **extend** children who are exceeding the ELGs. This clear differentiation ensures that all children in the group are exploring new ideas and concepts at a level appropriate to their stage of development. The Statutory Framework for the Early Years Foundation Stage states that (p.11) 'Practitioners must indicate whether children are meeting expected levels of development, or if they are exceeding expected levels, or not yet reaching expected levels. This is the EYFS Profile. The extension activities in this book are planned in line with the National Curriculum, ensuring that the children are building a firm foundation for Years 1 and 2.

◆ How to extend the activity throughout the week, with suggestions on how to deliver the activity as a **guided** session and ideas on how to encourage the children to work **independently**. The Statutory Framework for the Early Years Foundation Stage recognises that there is an important balance between activities led by children and activities led or guided by adults. It is important that 'each area of learning and development must be implemented through planned, purposeful play and through a mix of adult-led and child-initiated activity' (p.6, 2012). Each activity in this book includes guidance for practitioners as to how this balance can be achieved.

◆ Ideas for interactive display within the setting

◆ Ideas for parents and carers to use at home

Parents and carers as partners

Parents and carers are crucial in developing and supporting children's learning. This is recognised in the revised EYFS, and a key recommendation from the Tickell Review is that (p.18) '...the Government increases the emphasis within the EYFS on the role of parents and carers as partners in their children's learning...'. Indeed, the *Statutory Framework for the Early Years Foundation Stage* (March 2012) states that (p.2) 'Good parenting and high quality early learning together provide the foundation children need to make the most of their abilities and talents as they grow up.' The planning in this book includes an entire week based around inviting parents and carers into the setting to share in their children's curiosity and enthusiasm for learning. There are examples of how parents and carers can extend the learning at home, and ideas for giving parents and carers the opportunity not only to see what activities their children have been involved in, but also for them to join in alongside their children and to be really 'hands on'! One of the features which the EYFS seeks to provide (p.2, 2012) is 'partnership working between practitioners and with parents and/or carers.' This book recognises this as a priority.

Outdoor learning

Most of the activities are more than suitable to be engaged with outdoors as well as in a classroom – indeed for some of the activities it is necessary to be outdoors! And for some very messy, noisy or extensive activities I would recommend setting up outdoors to save carpets and soft furnishings and to minimise disruption to the rest of the learning environment. Hardly any of the activities require the children to sit and write in a formal situation. Where there is a suggestion to record, it is done either by an adult on a flipchart, children on individual whiteboards or pictorially, or through ICT, for example by the children using a digital camera or making a sound recording.

The revised curriculum

It is four years since the EYFS was introduced to provide a framework for all children in early years settings. The Tickell Report (2011) was carried out as an evaluation of the EYFS on children's outcomes and on those people working in the early years. One of the recommendations from the Tickell Report (2011) was that…

> …the assessment at the end of the EYFS, the EYFS Profile, should be significantly slimmed down and made much more manageable, based upon [my] 17 proposed new early learning goals…

The themes, principles and commitments of the EYFS remain the same, however the fourth theme, Learning and development has changed. This is the focus of our *Creative Planning in the EYFS* series. The *Statutory Framework for the Early Years Foundation Stage* (March 2012) states that one of the overarching principles which should shape practice in early years settings (p.3) is that 'children develop and learn in different ways and at different rates.' This book shows how topic-based activities can be provided in an exciting and practical way whilst still offering opportunities for all children at three levels of differentiation.

The research studied for the Tickell Report (2011) focuses on the concept that some aspects of development and learning include developing abilities, enabling children to be successful in all areas. These are referred to as 'prime areas of learning' and development. Other areas of learning are more specific to areas of knowledge and skills, these are known as 'specific areas of learning and development'.

Prime areas of learning and development

1. Communication and language

2. Physical development

3. Personal, social and emotional development

Specific areas of learning and development

1. Literacy

2. Mathematics

3. Understanding the world

4. Expressive arts and design

The activities in this book are planned around the four specific areas of learning and development – Literacy (formerly Communication, Language and Literacy), Mathematics (formerly Problem Solving, Reasoning and Numeracy), Understanding the world (formerly Knowledge and Understanding of the world) and Expressive Arts and Design (formerly Creative Development). However, the three prime areas are also covered through discussion, speaking and listening, turn taking and involvement in each task. It is essential that the prime and specific areas are planned for and experienced at the same time. They are not to be experienced chronologically but as an interwoven fabric of early years provision, as 'all areas of learning and development are important and inter-connected' (p.4, 2012).

Development in the prime areas has been called by neuroscientists 'experience expectant learning'. This is where a child's brain is ready to respond to interaction and stimulus, developing connections. Development in the specific areas however, will only develop when the need occurs, and includes cultural concepts such as learning to read and write, understand numbers, the number system and maps. This has been referred to as 'experience dependent learning'. (Hall, 2005).

The revisions made in the EYFS separate out the four strands of speaking, listening, reading and writing identified in the Rose Review (2006) into two areas: Communication and language (prime area) and Literacy (specific area). The Tickell Report (2011) explains this:

> …the development of communication and language skills happens during an optimum window of brain development and is experience expectant (therefore…prime)…whereas the acquisition of literacy skills is experience dependent since it can occur at any point in childhood or adulthood. (p.98)

As communication, language and literacy is so inextricably linked I have used ELGs from both these areas in the detailed differentiated activities.

Further reading

Hall, John (February 2005) **Neuroscience and Education – A review of the contribution of brain science to teaching and learning** Research Report No.121 Scottish Council for Research in Education

Rose, Jim (March 2006) **Independent review of the teaching of early reading** Final report Department for Education and Skills

Tickell, Clare (March 2011) **The Early Years: Foundations for life, health and learning** – An Independent Report on the Early Years Foundation Stage to Her Majesty's Government

Department for Education (March 2012) **Statutory Framework for the Early Years Foundation Stage** – Setting the standards for learning, development and care for children from birth to five

Effective learning, observation and assessment

Characteristics of Effective Learning

There are a number of learning characteristics which are evident in all seven areas of learning and development (p.7, 2012). These are not sequential, and it is not possible to identify particular ages or stages when they may be achieved. Learning characteristics include:

- **Playing and exploring** – engagement

- **Active learning** – motivation

- **Creating and thinking critically** – thinking

These learning characteristics should not be considered as an outcome which is summative, or marked in a 'tick list' manner. They represent processes, and may be observed during formative assessment.

Observation

It is crucial to observe children during their participation in these activities in order to assess whether they are working at an appropriate level and to work out their next steps in learning. The differentiation planned in the activity provides suitable challenge for all children.

Children can behave very differently during group, guided, independent and one-to-one opportunities. Some may be very quiet, and appear withdrawn or insecure during a group activity. However, given the opportunity to work with a close friend independently or at a self-chosen activity, a far more confident child may become apparent. Regular observation should therefore be a central part of good early years practice, ensuring that children are observed during different types of activity (guided, shared, self-chosen or independent), in differently sized groups with a range of children and at different times of day.

Sometimes it is useful to have a focus for observation such as an area of development or to discover the style of a child's learning, but at other times it is just as useful to observe the child for a period of time simply to discover what they are all about. If it appears that the child is making good progress, and is able to achieve what is required in an activity it is important to be aware of their next steps in learning. By always providing an opportunity for children to extend their learning they will continue to be interested and motivated, enjoying learning and finding out about new ideas. All of these are valuable personal characteristics which will be necessary throughout the whole of a child's life.

Assessment

The new EYFS will expect practicioners to make judgements as to whether a child is meeting, exceeding or emerging in relation to the Early Learning Goals (ELGs). In addition to their judgements, practicioners will need to make an assessment against the 3 characterisitcs of effective learning (see Observation record sheet page 57). As previously discussed, a child's learning characteristics are not suitable for summative assessment in a 'can they/can't they' manner. Rather, they should be thought of as part of a child's learning journey. It is for this reason that I am not recommending the use of a 'tick list' to record achievement of each learning characteristic. However, a simple observation record could include the characteristics observed during the observation and the context. This would build into a collection of evidence showing each child's strengths and areas for development. An example of an individual observation record of learning characteristics is provided on page 57.

The ELGs in both the prime and specific areas of learning are set at the expected level for a child nearing the end of FS2. Some children may be working towards achieving these goals and some may be exceeding them – it is the nature of any cohort of children. Indeed, there is likely to be discrepancy at times in a child's attainment towards the ELGs between areas of learning – a child rarely makes equal and comparative progress in all areas across a period of a year or more. It is not necessary to record in a numerical manner how a child achieves, but by highlighting the statement which most closely matches the attainment of the child, it is possible to identify their level of understanding and plan the next steps in progressing towards and exceeding the ELGs.

Using the group record sheets

The group record sheets on pages 58-61 can be used to show how a group of children are achieving at any one time – as a snapshot. It does not show progress over time or individual children's next steps but may be useful as a tool to show a co-ordinator or setting leader the strengths and areas for development of a cohort. It is not possible to fit all specific areas of learning onto one sheet so you may need to photocopy some back to back. There are a variety of record sheets here for both specific and prime areas of development. The group record sheet on page 58 for Communication and Language (prime) and Literacy (specific) also gives the opportunity to record achievement in all three areas on the same sheet, as some activities use ELGs from all of these areas. You may choose to use a traffic light system to record where children are in relation to each area of learning.

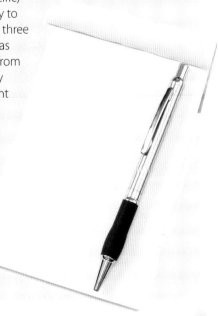

Autumn weather

Autumn everywhere

The children will be using their senses on an outdoor walk to identify signs of autumn and collect autumnal objects. They will extend their vocabulary by speaking, listening and describing what they encounter. Together they will collect words and phrases to write a class poem (adult may act as scribe).

Resources

★ As many adults as possible for the outdoor walk

★ Bags for collecting objects

★ Images of autumn to show the children

★ Simple non-fiction texts with pictures and information about autumn

★ Natural autumnal objects previously collected

★ A flipchart/whiteboard for an adult to act as scribe

★ Pre-cut leaf shapes on coloured paper for the independent activity

★ Pencils

Storybooks

★ *Tales from Percy's Park – After the Storm* by Nick Butterworth and other *Percy* stories about Autumn and the changing seasons.

Observation and assessment

Communication and Language	Expected statements (ELGs)
Speaking	Children express themselves effectively, showing awareness of listeners' needs.
	They use past, present and future forms accurately when talking about events that have happened or are to happen in the future.

Literacy	Expected statements (ELGs)
Reading	They demonstrate understanding when talking with others about what they have read.

Key vocabulary

- autumn
- winter
- spring
- summer
- season
- weather
- green
- yellow
- brown
- orange

- smooth
- rough
- shiny
- dull
- crispy
- crackly
- crunchy
- spiky
- conker
- leaf

- tree
- shell
- nut
- pinecone
- nature
- natural

Safety first!

Make sure children:
★ *check with an adult before they pick up things from the floor*
★ *do not pull things directly from trees or plants*
★ *do not eat anything they find.*

What to do

Discuss the four seasons and how they run in a cycle. Briefly talk about the main characteristics of each, highlighting autumn as the current season. Explain to the children that they are going outside to look at the weather and search for natural objects to discover what changes occur during autumn. Make sure the children are clear about the safety requirements (see flash). Go on the walk making sure you have a high ratio of adults to children to make the activity more successful, as the children get to ask questions, talk about objects and events they observe and use new vocabulary. If you are in a built environment and it is difficult to find natural objects, focus on the weather, how the children feel and how they and other people they see must dress for the temperature. Use the key vocabulary where relevant.

On return to the classroom, gather together any objects found and share what the children saw, heard and experienced outside. Demonstrate choosing an object from the collection (e.g. a spiky conker shell or a dry, crispy leaf) and pass it around the group. When each child holds the object they are to say something about it for example, finding an adjective to describe it; where it came from; what it reminds them of; how it has changed. If it proved difficult to find natural objects have some already in the classroom in a 'here's some I found earlier' style! Encourage all children to contribute where possible. The adult can act as scribe, recording their ideas on the flipchart. Use the children's words to make a simple group poem in a list format, beginning 'Autumn is…'

If this is to be a guided activity…

…then the children can work together with an adult to create a list of adjectives describing either a particular natural object or describing features of Autumn, e.g. 'Autumn is… a shiny conker/a crispy leaf/a spiky shell/a foggy day'. Although this idea can be demonstrated in a large group, it is more successful in smaller groups of between 4–8 children as they don't have to sit and wait so long for their turn, and can be encouraged not to repeat a previous word.

If this is to be an independent activity…

…then show the children where the collection of objects will be, and explain that sometime during the week they are to choose one of the objects. Working with a partner, they are to pass it backwards and forwards between themselves, each time saying a descriptive word or phrase.

To extend this invite children to choose a leaf from the pre-cut shapes and attempt to write their favourite word or phrase onto the leaf shape independently. Attach these to a display board with a tree outline.

To support or extend

To support, make the ratio of adults to children as low as possible: either one-to-one or one-to-two. Give the children a limited number of objects, and make simple word cards for the children to match, such as green, brown, orange, smooth, shiny, crispy, crackly, spiky. Give each child a card. Hold up an object, if their word describes that object they must stand and say their word. Repeat what they say in a clear sentence: 'Yes, well done, this conker is shiny and brown!'.

To extend the more able children, encourage them to complete the extension in the independent activity above, recording their ideas on leaf outlines. You can further investigate the children's understanding and thought processes by encouraging them to independently sort the natural objects, using their own criteria. Provide two or three baskets or sorting hoops for them to sort objects into. Prompt them to put the objects into the baskets or hoops and then explain to their partner or an adult their reasoning behind the choices. To elicit further discussion, an adult could sort the objects and ask the children to write on a whiteboard what they think the labels of the groups should be, e.g. spiky/not spiky; brown/not brown; leaves/not leaves. Link the idea to mathematics activities and the use of Venn diagrams.

Ideas for interactive display

Put up some pictures of autumn animals, weather and scenes. Provide some baskets for the children to keep collections of natural autumn objects, along with sticky labels to allow the children to record how they have chosen to sort the objects. If possible, put the digital camera out for the children to take photographs of autumn scenes or objects which cannot be brought indoors.

Parents and carers as partners

At home, go for a walk together and collect anything that the child finds interesting. Often it won't be a natural object – a piece of litter or a lost button. When you return home with your bag of treasure spend some time looking at it together: talk about where you found it, what it is and who/where it came from. You could also use your objects to make a collage picture.

Autumn weather

Windy sailing boats

The children will be using different shapes to make sails, and putting small toy animals in the boat to see how many of them the boat will carry. They will be practising counting, cutting and making, talking with their friends and taking turns at sailing their boats!

Observation and assessment

Mathematics	Expected statements (ELGs)
Numbers	Children count reliably with numbers from 1 to 20, place them in order and say which number is one more or one less than a given number.
Shape, space and measures	Children use everyday language to talk about size, weight, capacity, position, distance, time and money to compare quantities and objects and to solve problems.

Resources

★ Pictures of sailing boats

★ Small foil/plastic trays of different shapes and sizes (base of the boat)

★ Lolly sticks (masts)

★ Sticky tape

★ Plasticine or play dough (to attach the mast to the base of boat)

★ Card either cut into sail shapes or pre-drawn with squares, rectangles and triangles for sails

★ Small toy animals

★ Water tray

★ Clipboards

Storybooks

★ *Who Sank The Boat?* by Pamela Allen

★ *Mr Gumpy's Outing* by John Burningham

Key vocabulary

- sail
- mast
- square
- triangle
- rectangle
- float
- sink
- estimate

To support or extend

To support, give the children a pre-cut sail shape and help them to attach the mast. Let them play with the boat, loading animals until it sinks! Use simple words such as more/less, how many altogether? and count in order using the number names.

To extend the more able children, encourage them to estimate how many small toy animals they think they can place in their boat before it will sink. Test out their theory: were they correct? Using this information, can they try with differently sized animals? Introduce the concept of predicting an event before it happens, encouraging the children to use the clipboards and paper available to draw and record their predictions and findings. These can be kept as examples of emergent mathematics and used in discussions later.

Ideas for interactive display

Provide a selection of containers and different toy animals for the children to investigate. Encourage them to consider the different sizes and shapes of container along with the different animals, recording their ideas and predictions onto small whiteboards. Let them use a water tray outside to test their predictions.

What to do

Safety first!

This activity must be wholly supervised – children can drown in only an inch of water.

Explain to the children they are going to make a sailing boat and blow it along the water tray to see if it will sail. Show them some images of sailing boats, talk about the shape of sails. Introduce the key vocabulary, showing the children the different sail shapes and naming them. Demonstrate constructing the boat, particularly how to use sticky tape to attach the straw to the sail, and how to press the straw into the Plasticine so that it stands straight. Encourage the children to gently place their boat into the water tray to ensure it will balance and float before they begin to blow it along.

If this is to be a guided activity...

...then the children can work together with an adult to construct their boats and sail them together as a group. The role of the adult is to encourage the children to use some key vocabulary when playing with their boats, and also to develop and secure the prime areas of development of PSED and Communication and language.

If this is to be an independent activity...

...then show the children where the box of resources will be, and explain that they can try this activity sometime during the week. Encourage them to record their findings independently by using the clipboards and paper to draw or write. Keep these as examples of emergent mathematics to discuss with the children later.

Parents and carers as partners

At home, play in the sink, bath or paddling pool with plastic containers, spoons, sieves and strainers to float, fill, sink and spill differently sized 'boats'. Talk about full, empty, more and less when playing, guessing how many spoons will fill the 'boat' before it sinks.

Autumn weather

Blowing along!

The children will be using an electric fan to blow objects along a table. They will be using comparative language, measuring the distance travelled. They will be speaking in a familiar group, talking about their ideas, and choosing the resources they need for the activity.

Observation and assessment

Understanding the world	Expected statements (ELGs)
The world	Children know about similarities and differences in relation to places, objects, materials and living things.
Technology	Children recognise that a range of technology is used in places such as homes and schools. They select and use technology for particular purposes.

Resources

Safety first!
Demonstrate how to turn the fan on and off with the switch but tell children never to touch the plug, wire or to move the table.

★ Electric fan with enclosed blades

★ Table with lining paper

★ Pictures of hairdryers and wind turbines

★ Selection of familiar objects: balloon, tissue, straw, book, mug, brick, include some things which roll: ball, car, cardboard tube

★ Clipboards with paper and pencils for children to record their results

Storybooks

★ *Elmer and the Wind* by David McGee

★ *The Blue Balloon* and *Kipper's Balloon* both by Mick Inkpen

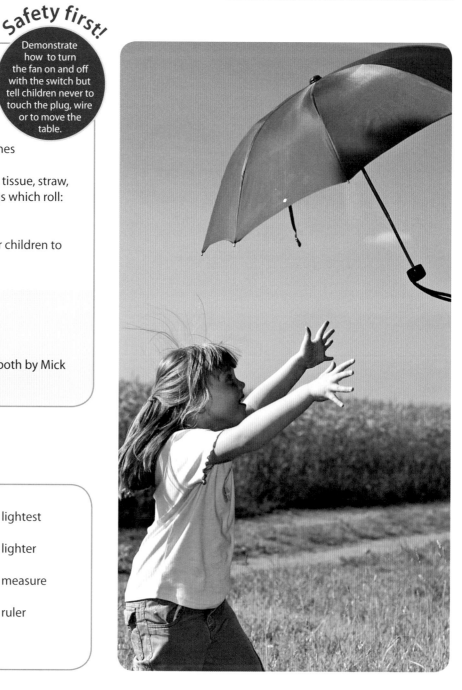

Key vocabulary

- fan
- blow
- air
- wind
- further
- furthest
- heavy
- heaviest
- heavier
- light
- lightest
- lighter
- measure
- ruler

What to do

Explain to the children that they are going to explore how different objects can be moved by air. Set up the electric fan on a table against a wall, plugged in so no wires are visible or trailing protecting the wire, plug and socket from small fingers! Tape lining paper to the table to allow children to record directly onto the surface.

Show them the fan and explain how it moves air by turning really quickly. Ask the children if they have a fan at home; draw parallels with hairdryers and wind turbines and show pictures of these. Introduce the key vocabulary. Demonstrate putting an object in front of the fan (e.g. the balloon) and asking the children to predict what will happen when the fan is turned on. Were they correct? Can they think of any other objects that will move in the same way? Encourage them to select objects from around the classroom to use in front of the fan, giving reasons for their choices.

If this is to be a guided activity…

…then the children can work together with an adult to explore the way different objects behave in front of the fan. The role of the adult is to encourage the children to use some key vocabulary when they are playing, and to begin to predict how objects will behave, giving reasons for their ideas.

If this is to be an independent activity…

…then show the children where the fan table is set up, and explain that they can try this activity sometime during the week. Encourage them to record their findings independently. Children could draw and write directly on the paper covered tabletop, or use the clipboards. Children needing more support could simply place the objects in a line in the order of distance they blew, for the adult to come and look at. Keep any examples of recording as evidence of emergent mathematics.

To support or extend

To support, give the children two or three objects with very different characteristics of size and weight. Work with them, encouraging them to handle the objects and make a simple prediction: 'The balloon will blow right off the table! But the book is very heavy so it won't move'. Record their findings by simply placing the items into one of two hoops on the floor: Too heavy to move/Blown by the fan. Can they begin to predict the outcome before testing?

To extend the more able children encourage them to estimate how far the objects will move from the fan. Can they place the objects in a line showing their prediction? Record this line with a digital camera before testing out their theory, were they correct? Take another photograph to compare their findings. Encourage the children to use the clipboards available to draw and record their predictions and findings. To add more mathematical opportunities draw a ruler line along the paper-covered table so that children can begin to record and compare length using standard measures.

This information could also be shown to the class in a traditional bar graph on the whiteboard, by asking the children to simply drag the icons to different places on the y (vertical) axis *. Extend understanding by asking questions such as: Which object blew the furthest? Which object do you think was the heaviest? Why?

Ideas for interactive display

On the wall display pictures and photographs of items that use air or wind power, e.g. a hot air balloon, a sail boat, a windmill, a wind turbine, a kite. Label the pictures clearly. Provide some drinking straws for the children to blow through and different items for them to blow along, e.g. a feather, a ping pong ball, a balloon, tissue paper, and let them investigate the properties of the different materials.

Parents and carers as partners

At home, go for a windy walk together! Children love wind, and will delight in letting go of leaves, grass or petals to watch them blow away. Take a kite if you have one, and let your child experience the pull of the wind. Explain that this is how the sail on a boat works.

Bar graphs can be made easier to interpret by placing them on their side to show the y axis (in this case distance blown by the fan) horizontally, left to right.

Autumn weather

Wind whirlers and twirlers!

The children will be making whirlers and twirlers to move in the wind, experimenting with the colour, design, shape and form of a variety of materials of different textures and characteristics. They will be able to make music and dance, and use their own ideas to create movements and music.

Observation and assessment

Expressive arts and design	Expected statements (ELGs)
Exploring and using media and materials	Children sing songs, make music and dance, and experiment with ways of changing them. They safely use and explore a variety of materials, tools and techniques, experimenting with colour, design, texture, form and function.
Being imaginative	Children use what they have learnt about media and materials in original ways, thinking about users and purposes. They represent their own ideas, thoughts and feelings through design and technology, art, music, dance, role-play and stories.

Resources

To make the whirler/twirler:

★ Sticks/lengths of dowelling between 30 cm and 50 cm long

★ Ribbons, crêpe paper strips, cellophane and tissue paper all of different width, length, colour and texture

★ Sticky tape to attach streamers to the stick

For the dance activity:

★ Assorted musical instruments

★ CD and player with music suitable for dancing and movement

Storybooks and film clips

★ *Mrs Mopple's Washing Line* by Anita Hewitt and Robert Broomfield

★ *Mirandy and Brother Wind* by Patricia C. McKissack

★ Look for online film clips clips showing gymnastic ribbon dancing

Key vocabulary

• join	• fast	• turn
• measure	• high	• twirl
• long	• low	• whirl
• short	• up	• move
• wide	• down	• loud
• narrow	• blow	• soft
• slow	• wave	

What to do

Explain to the children that they are going to make a wind twirler: a stick with various trailing streamers that they can run, jump, move and dance with. Show them the different materials that they can choose from to attach to their stick. Draw attention to the similar properties of the streamer strips: they are light, floaty and will blow in the wind. Remind the children how flags and washing blow and wave in the wind. Show a film clip online of rhythmic gymnastic ribbon dancing to the children. Introduce key vocabulary, choosing different items from the resource list to demonstrate the meanings of the words.

Demonstrate by selecting strips of streamer and attaching these to the end of the stick with the tape. Encourage the children to give reasons for their choices, and to consider colour, texture, shape and form before attaching any streamers.

For the follow-up dance activity provide the children with a selection of instruments and allow them to investigate different sounds and ways of making music. If you have a CD player which the children can use independently then allow them to play music to dance to, moving their bodies and wind twirlers in a variety of ways similar to those of the rhythmic gymnast seen on the film clips.

If this is to be a guided activity…

…then the children can work together with an adult to choose a selection of resources to make a wind twirler, describing the properties of the materials they have chosen and giving reasons for their selections. The dance could be a group activity, such as a PE lesson, provide some guidance: high in the air; move slowly and smoothly; twirl around and around when the music moves quickly to structure the dancing.

If this is to be an independent activity…

…then show the children where the box of resources will be, and explain that they can try this activity sometime during the week. Ask them to think carefully about the choices they will make and maybe limit them to, for example, only six pieces of streamer to construct their wind twirler. Leave the basket of instruments for the children to explore, choosing different sounds to move to. If it is possible for the children to operate the CD player independently then they can perform and dance to music, moving imaginatively.

To support or extend

To support, work either one-to-one or one-to-two to ensure that the children are using some of the simple key vocabulary accurately and purposefully. Limit the number of streamer strips they can choose either by colour, number or both: Choose four red strips to join to your stick. Help them with the sticky tape if required. In the dance session give short clear instructions to the children on how to move: Run quickly; wave your wind twirler in front of you; walk slowly backwards; twirl your twirler on the ground.

To extend the more able children, encourage them to work independently to create their wind twirlers, explore and choose different musical sounds and create distinctive movements to match the music played. In pairs, they could experiment with moving in a mirror-symmetry style, copying their partner's movements or leading a line of children around in a 'follow the leader' style, travelling high and low across the space. Using each other as a critical audience they could say what they liked and did not like about each performance, and make changes to their own work where necessary to improve it.

Ideas for interactive display

Attach a washing line between two points which the children can walk around. Provide pegs and a variety of strips of different types of paper and fabric which the children can peg to the line. Encourage them to blow the different strips, investigating which blow easily and which need a lot of wind power! Show them how to order the strips to show their results.

Parents and carers as partners

At home, let your child play with scarves and pieces of material of different sizes and textures to run, jump, twirl and twist around. Look at how the fabric moves, play some music on the radio and let them move in time with it.

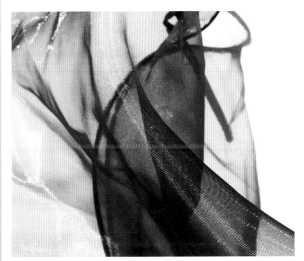

Autumn animals

Spikey poetry

The children will be looking carefully at hedgehogs in books and in film clips, and extending their vocabulary by describing hedgehogs in a poem.

Resources

* ★ Pictures of hedgehogs (laminated)

* ★ Simple non-fiction books about hedgehogs

* ★ Microphone and recording equipment

Storybooks and film clips

* ★ *Hedgehogs* episode from *Come Outside* with Mabel and Pippin is really useful to give the children a little background knowledge (BBC)

* ★ *Winter Hedgehog* by Ann and Reg Cartwright

* ★ *Ouch!* by Ragnhild Scamell

* ★ Online film clips of hedgehogs in their natural environment: try the RSPCA and National Geographic websites

Key vocabulary

• hedgehog	• roll	• scurry
• hoglet	• snuffle	• spiky
• spine	• sniff	• prickly
• ball	• scamper	• sharp

Observation and assessment

Communication and Language	Expected statements (ELGs)
Listening and attention	Children listen attentively in a range of situations. They give their attention to what others say and respond appropriately, while engaged in another activity.
Understanding	They answer 'how' and 'why' questions about their experiences and in response to stories or events.
Speaking	They develop their own narratives and explanations by connecting ideas or events.

Literacy	Expected statements (ELGs)
Writing	Children use their phonic knowledge to write words in ways which match their spoken sounds. They also write some irregular common words. They write simple sentences which can be read by themselves and others. Some words are spelt correctly and others are phonetically plausible.

What to do

Explain to the children that they are going to learn about hedgehogs. Watch the *Come Outside* episode if possible, look at the film clips online and pass the pictures and photographs around for the children to see. Discuss what the children already know about hedgehogs: has anyone actually seen one? Encourage the children to listen carefully to each other when speaking. Use the key vocabulary where relevant, modelling the correct way to put the words into a sentence.

Ask the children to think of words to describe a hedgehog, and act as a scribe to write them on a large sheet of paper. Let the children help you with sounding out the words to spell, encouraging them to use their phonic knowledge. The more able children could write their describing words onto sticky notes and add them onto the collection of words. Explain to the children that they are to choose a describing word from the collected ideas and put it into a sentence as a simile: *Spiky* like a conker shell/*Rolled up* like a ball/*Snuffly* like a rabbit's nose/*Scurrying* like a little mouse. Encourage all of the children to contribute where possible, but if a child chooses not to speak this time explain that they can simply listen to the others. Continue to act as scribe, recording their phrases on the flipchart. Translate the children's words into a simple descriptive poem.

If this is to be a guided activity…

…then the children can work together with an adult to create a collection of words and phrases to describe a hedgehog. Talk about what it reminds them of; ask them to draw parallels with other objects and experiences. The words could be written on individual hand-shaped labels and displayed by the children to make a large hedgehog picture on the wall. See page 24.

If this is to be an independent activity…

…then show the children where the collection of pictures and simple non-fiction books about hedgehogs will be, and explain that sometime during the week they are to take time to look at them and think of words to describe the hedgehogs in the pictures. Provide a microphone and a method of recording the children's voices to allow them to record their thoughts.

To support, collect a selection of everyday objects with spikes or spines, for example hairbrushes and combs, Sticklebricks and other similar construction toys, a bundle of sharp pencil crayons, dry spaghetti, natural objects such as pinecones, conker shells and holly leaves. Allow the children to look at these and handle them carefully. Show the children the pictures of the hedgehogs and encourage them to draw parallels between the objects they can feel and the images of the hedgehogs. Model the use of key vocabulary in simple sentences: The hedgehog looks spiky like the hairbrush. The children could sort or group the objects according to their own chosen criteria, or place in groups according to directions from the adult. With support they could write a describing word onto a small whiteboard or card label.

To extend the more able children, read together some of the fiction storybooks featuring hedgehogs that are recommended above. Talk about some of the problems encountered by the hedgehog (not hibernating during winter, being so spiky that objects are caught on their spines). Discuss why these things have happened and how they were resolved in the stories. Encourage the children to think of other problems a hedgehog might have – be creative! Draw three very simple sketches to show the beginning, middle and end of the story plan for the children and ask them to write a few simple sentences underneath each picture to tell the story, or act as scribe for them.

Ideas for interactive display

Create a 'texture table' where the children can explore the texture of different items. Begin with a collection of spiky items similar to the hedgehog, e.g. hairbrushes and combs, Sticklebricks, conker shells and holly leaves. Show the children how to close their eyes, pick up an item and try to guess what it is simply by feeling. Extend the texture table by introducing other textures, e.g. smooth or bumpy.

Parents and carers as partners

At home, look for signs of animals in your local area. Look on the ground for tracks or footprints, or any plants that may have been nibbled by creatures. If you have the opportunity, put out water and food for birds to encourage them to visit your local park or garden.

Autumn animals

Animal footprints

The children will be sorting and grouping different animals' footprints, using these to count in groups in a simple multiplication as addition activity.

Observation and assessment

Mathematics	Expected statements (ELGs)
Numbers	Children count reliably with numbers from 1 to 20, place them in order and say which number is one more or one less than a given number. Using quantities and objects, they add and subtract two single-digit numbers and count on or back to find the answer. They solve problems, including doubling, halving and sharing.

Key vocabulary

- how many?
- more
- less
- one more
- one less
- another
- repeat
- number labels up to ten
- forward
- backwards
- group
- twos
- threes
- fours
- fives

Resources

★ Examples of different animal footprints – look for images on the internet

★ Paper towels or sugar paper

★ Pairs and sets of toy animals

★ Potatoes cut in half

★ Paint, sponges and trays

★ Large pieces of paper – lining wallpaper is ideal and cheap

Storybooks

★ *Footprints in the Snow* and *Footprints in the Sand* by Cynthia Benjamin and Jacqueline Rogers

★ *Whose Footprint Is That? (Animal Detectives* series) by Jacqui Brown

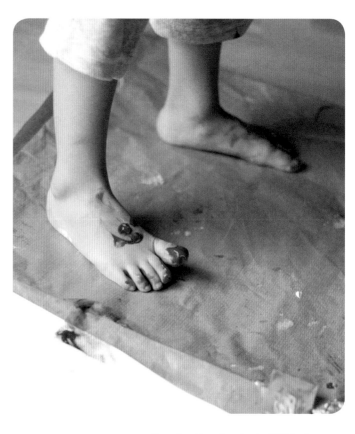

What to do

Explain to the children that all animals, including people leave tracks in snow, mud or water when they walk. This is how people track and follow animals in the wild to find out more about them. Show them some examples from the internet. Allow the children to wet their own bare foot and make a print upon a piece of paper towel or sugar paper. Draw around it when wet so that they are able to count their toes in the print even when it has dried. (You could of course use paint for this activity but that is a whole teaching session in itself!)

Demonstrate counting the toes on different types of footprint, and encourage the children to use the toy animals to sort and group into collections with two toes, such as deer, three toes such as birds, four toes such as dogs and foxes and five toes such as hedgehogs. Draw a single deer print on a piece of paper (such as a piece of lining paper) and ask the children: How many toes altogether? Write '2' underneath it. Draw another deer print next to the first: How many toes now altogether? Write '4' underneath. Continue in this way, explaining that as the deer walks along it leaves a longer trail of footprints, and we can count along this line in groups of two when counting how many toes altogether. Keep checking that the children know and understand the difference between how many *footprints* and how many *toes*. Encourage them to move whilst counting in twos: ask all the children to stand in a 'follow my leader' line, each time the adult points to a footprint the children step forwards saying 'Two!' Then another point, another step and 'Four!' When the children are able to count in twos by rote this can become a marching activity. Depending upon the age and ability of the children you can repeat this activity with other footprints, counting in threes, fours and fives.

If this is to be a guided activity…

…then the children can work together with an adult to make a long track with printed footprints. Cut out a deer cloven hoof footprint (with two toes) in a potato and use it to make a stamp. Show the children how to dip it in paint, stamp it onto the paper and write a numeral next to it. Provide number lines colour coded in multiples to help them.

If this is to be an independent activity…

…then show the children where the roll of paper will be and explain that they can try this activity sometime this week. Encourage them to use the potato stamps to print onto the paper, counting the toes each time and recording the numeral. For different abilities of children provide different potato stamps – the more able could extend to counting in threes, fours and fives.

To support, give the children a stamp with one single 'monster's footprint' without any toes on it, and ask them to stamp it along the roll of paper in a line. Count aloud with each stamping action up to a number appropriate for the children. Give the children a number card each and ask them firstly to read aloud the number they have. Then give them support to order themselves, firstly into a line of ascending order then help them to place their cards down in the correct order alongside the footprints. Count forwards and backwards along this line, pointing to each numeral when saying it.

To extend the more able children, encourage them to investigate how many toes there would be in a pair of footprints from different animals. Tell them that they can use the paper, potato stamps, counters and number cards in any way they like to firstly explore the answers and then show their findings to an adult. When observing the children working try to ask questions to consolidate their existing knowledge and then take them further, posing open questions such as: What if…? Does that mean that…? Would it work for…? If appropriate, use mathematical vocabulary such as repeat, groups of, multiply and add.

Ideas for interactive display

Put up a washing line, laminate and number some footprints. Show the children how to peg them up in the correct order. If you make the odd and even numbered feet different colours the children can begin to look at patterns in number. Provide card, scissors and pencils so that the children can make footprints of their own, draw on a number (e.g. their age, house number) and attach it to the line.

Parents and carers as partners

At home, go for a walk and look at the footprints left behind by different people's shoes and boots when they walk through a puddle. If you can find some mud, practise stamping some muddy prints and look at how the ridges are raised under the soles of wellington boots.

Autumn animals

Nuts about nuts!

The children will be making small world environments using collected natural materials – in the sand tray or outdoors. To extend, they will use a simple grid reference to search for buried acorns, and make a map of their findings.

Resources

★ Sand tray with a shallow layer of damp sand

★ Collection of natural objects: twigs, grass, stones, pebbles, leaves etc.

★ Acorns

★ String

★ Stickers

★ Paper with very large squares (drawn or folded)

★ A small model animal (preferably a squirrel!)

★ Teaspoon

★ Digital camera

Storybooks

★ *The Nutty Nut Chase* by Kathryn White

★ *Busy Animals – Learning about animals in Autumn* by Lisa Bullard

Key vocabulary

• nut	• bury	• environment
• acorn	• dig	• grid
• find	• winter	• natural object
• lost	• map	

Observation and assessment

Understanding the world	Expected statements (ELGs)
The world	Children know about similarities and differences in relation to places, objects, materials and living things. They talk about the features of their own immediate environment and how environments might vary from one another

What to do

Read the children a story about a squirrel that needs to bury his acorns under the ground to save as a food source. Explain that this is what some animals do in the autumn, saving food until they need it. Draw parallels with humans and their harvesting activities. Tell the children that they are going to make a small world environment in a sand tray using natural objects. A previous activity for this session could be to go and collect suitable natural materials to make a small world such as grass to replicate a field, stones for rocks, small twigs with leaves attached for trees and so on. Show them how to place their objects into the tray making a natural environment for the squirrel to explore. Demonstrate hiding an acorn under the layer of sand, showing them where it is placed and how to smooth over the sand layer afterwards so that no one else can tell the hiding place. Encourage them to ask you questions to find the location such as: Is it near to the trees? Is it closer to the big stone or the smaller stone? Listen carefully to the language children are using – are they able to differentiate between the natural materials and the position of items in the tray?

Attach one piece of string lengthways over the tray with sticky tape and a shorter piece over the tray widthways, creating a grid of four squares. Use stickers to label the squares with letters A and B and numbers 1 and 2 in the style of a simple grid reference. Show the children how to refer to each square area, using a small toy (preferably a squirrel!) to move along the edge of the bottom squares (A and B) before moving up into the numbered squares (1 and 2). Ask questions to check that the children understand the way that the grid references work. Allow the children to use a combination of the grid references and detailed questions to find the exact location of the hidden acorn, finally unearthing it with a teaspoon! Allow them to bury the acorn whilst your back is turned and let them delight in your bafflement as 'the adult' tries to locate the acorn treasure!

If this is to be a guided activity…

…then the children can work together to make a small world natural environment in a small tray drawer – it does not have to be in the large sand tray. Attach the string in the same way as before, extending to one piece length ways and two pieces top to bottom, making a grid of ABC/1 2. Label the squares as before, using stickers, and then ensure all the children can ask and answer questions about locating items on the 'map'. If you bury a handful of acorns it is possible for each child to find one. Alternatively, they can work in pairs to find each other's.

If this is to be an independent activity…

…then explain to the children that there is a box of natural objects near to the sand tray and that they can use these, and anything else they find, to make a natural 'squirrel world'. Show them how to attach the string over the tray (already cut to size and provided, along with sticky tape) to make the grid and to label the squares with stickers. Let them play hiding the acorns for their friends and then asking questions about finding them, encouraging the use of accurate positional language and detailed reference to the natural objects and grid references. If you provide a digital camera the children can photograph the small worlds they have created.

To support or extend

To support, work in a very small group to explore hiding things and asking questions to find its location. This activity works particularly well outdoors, where you may give the children large pine cones to represent the nut, and ask them questions using positional language and details from the environment around them to find their chosen hidden location: Is it near the big tree? Is it underneath the climbing frame? To check their knowledge and use of this vocabulary you can reverse the activity by telling children where to hide their pine cone: Put it on something flat. Hide it underneath something green. Children absolutely love the sense of excitement when hiding and searching for objects!

To extend the more able children encourage them to create a thoughtfully planned natural environment, giving reasons for their choices whilst designing and making. Following this, extend further if appropriate by making a paper map of the small world created. This is simply done by folding a plain sheet of paper into the required numbers of grid squares and then by showing the children how to focus on one square at a time to draw the objects only in that square. Encourage the use of accurate colour and scale of objects. They can label their grid squares as the sand trays are labelled. If they are competent at this they could record their treasure locations onto the paper maps, or play a very simplified game of coordinate battleships

Ideas for interactive display

Put up examples of maps on the wall, showing different types, colours, and scale. Provide plain and squared paper of different sizes for the children to design and illustrate their own maps and plans. A tray of sand, acorns and other natural materials could be put alongside the display for children to record their maps in 3D!

Parents and carers as partners

At home, play games such as 'battleships' simply using pencil and paper. Let your child look at maps with you: as well as road atlases many public places (such as shopping centres) have simple picture maps on large boards, often with a 'You are here!' arrow. Take five minutes to look at these each time you and your child see one.

Autumn animals

Handy hedgehogs

The children will be printing their handprints in different coloured paints and cutting them out to make paper hedgehogs.

Resources

* Ready mixed 'squeezy' paint in autumn colours (red, brown, yellow, orange etc.)

* Coloured paper in autumn colours, cut into rectangles of child's hand size

* Trays big enough to press a child's hand into

* Scissors

* Black card or paper

* Bowl of warm soapy water and towel

Storybooks

* *Hedgehog Howdedo* by Lynley Dodd

* *Hodge the Hedgehog* by Amy Sparkes

Key vocabulary

handprint	print	cut
fingers	repeat	shape
paint	colour	scissors
press	mix	

Observation and assessment

Expressive arts and design	Expected statements (ELGs)
Exploring and using media and materials	They safely use and explore a variety of materials, tools and techniques, experimenting with colour, design, texture, form and function.
Being imaginative	Children use what they have learnt about media and materials in original ways, thinking about uses and purposes.

What to do

Explain to the children that they are going to make handprints in different colours to create a picture of a hedgehog. Show them the paint trays and discuss what colours would be most appropriate. Introduce the idea of warm colours and cold colours, watery colours, hot, dry colours and lush growing colours. Let the children look at the tubes of ready mixed paint and let them sort them into warm, autumn colours and those which are not. Hopefully you will end up with reds, oranges, yellows and browns!

Introduce the key vocabulary, demonstrating how the children should press their hands into the paint ensuring that all their palm and fingers are covered in paint, before pressing onto paper – fingers splayed. Practise splaying fingers together as a group before the activity, drawing the children's attention to the fact that the spiky fingertips will mimic the spines of the hedgehogs when they are cut out. Let the children make two or three differently coloured handprints each. Encourage them to give reasons for their choices of colours in paint and paper. Have a bowl of warm, soapy water and a towel ready to wash and dry hands immediately. When the handprints are dry they can be cut out, either by an adult or by the child as a further creative exercise.

Cut out a simple hedgehog head and body outline from black card or paper, and help the children to attach the handprints in the manner of spiky spines. If this final stage is done by the children then each hedgehog will look slightly different from the others, and together they make a marvellous scene, snuffling about in the leaves at the bottom of an autumn display.

If this is to be a guided activity…

…then the children can work together with an adult to create the handprints, giving reasons for their colour choices and thinking through their choices, e.g. 'I won't put yellow handprints onto yellow paper because I won't be able to see it!' When cutting out, it is a useful opportunity to sit alongside a child and observe how they approach cutting with scissors: do they know how to hold them, can they turn the paper with the other hand, are they left handed?

If this is to be an independent activity…

…then be prepared for a lot of handpainted walls, tables, taps and sinks! Alternatively, provide the children with a box of resources containing an assortment of autumn coloured paper of different textures and sizes, pencils, crayons, chalks and felt tips in similar colours and explain that they can use these items this week to make cut outs of their hands. Demonstrate to the group how to draw around their own hand, cut it out carefully and decorate it however they like. Have some images of hands decorated with henna in intricate Mendhi patterns to stimulate their imaginations.

To support or extend

To support, encourage the children to consider the colours of objects around them. To begin, simply sort the construction bricks out into separate colours, choose pegs of the same colour to make peg board patterns or thread the beads onto colours of the same string. These are all excellent activities to hone fine motor skills. When the children can differentiate between colours of the same item begin a colour hunt, for example placing a red sheet of paper on the floor and asking the children to look around the setting, collecting any items that are red. Talk about the different shades of red that have been collected, but reiterate that they are all still red. Repeat with other autumnal colours such as orange, yellow and brown. Display these colour collections together, and explain to the children that blue or green items would not belong in this set. Independently the children could use the objects in the colour collections to create a representation of a person, a robot or a car.

To extend the more able children, encourage them to create coloured handprints, squeezing a different coloured paint at each end of the tray before putting their hands in, looking how the paint mixes in the centre of the print and makes an entirely new colour.

With a collection of dry handprints of different colours can they sort or group the prints into a colour chart of their own devising, perhaps from light to dark tones, or warm and cool colours. Give reasons for their choices. Have any of their friends made the same colour, or a colour they prefer? Which is their favourite handprint, and why?

Ideas for interactive display

Provide lots of different gloves and mittens for the children to investigate and pair up. Include those for a variety of purposes, e.g. rubber gloves for washing up, gardening gloves, skiing mittens, baby scratch mitts, latex gloves and oven gloves. Encourage the children to sort these according to their own critera, such as size or purpose.

Parents and carers as partners

At home, making wet prints outdoors is a fun activity which leaves little mess! Give your child a bucket of water and a paintbrush and let them go and make wet handprints and paint letter shapes on the dry ground. As soon as the sun shines it disappears, and they can paint and print all over again!

Autumn food and harvest

Exploring fruit and vegetables

The children will be writing a 'Thank you for...' poem, listing favourite fruit and vegetables. They will be closely observing, smelling and tasting different fruits and vegetables in order to describe them and their qualities.

Resources

* Basket containing selection of fruit and vegetables including favourites and some that the children are not so familiar with

* Knife and chopping board

* Sticky notes/blank word cards

* Flipchart and pens

* Microphone and recording equipment

Safety first!
Ensure that none of the children have allergies to any of the foods being investigated.

Storybooks

* *Oliver's Vegetables* and *Oliver's Fruit Salad* by Vivian French

* *P is for Pumpkin – God's Harvest Alphabet* by Kathy-Jo Wargin

Key vocabulary

* names of the selected fruit and vegetables

ripe	skin	colour words
crisp	flesh	
juicy/juice	pips	harvest
soft	seeds	
peel	texture	

Observation and assessment

Communication and Language	Expected statements (ELGs)
Listening and attention	Children listen attentively in a range of situations. They give their attention to what others say and respond appropriately, while engaged in another activity.
Understanding	They answer 'how' and 'why' questions about their experiences and in response to stories or events.
Speaking	They develop their own narratives and explanations by connecting ideas or events.

Literacy	Expected statements (ELGs)
Writing	Children use their phonic knowledge to write words in ways which match their spoken sounds. They also write some irregular common words. They write simple sentences which can be read by themselves and others. Some words are spelt correctly and others are phonetically plausible.

What to do

Discuss the time of the year, and explain that in many parts of the world autumn is the time when food is harvested from the trees and fields. Ask the children to share any experiences they have of this with you – draw parallels with Oliver's grandparents in the storybooks listed above. Talk about the festival of harvest, explaining that this is when we give thanks for the food we have. Explain to the children that they are going to look at some different fruits and vegetables, using all their senses to explore the smell, taste, look and feel of the fruit. Use the key vocabulary where relevant, trying to elicit further detail from the children in their comments: It's red… like a shiny berry. I think it tastes fresh…like grass smells. Pass around some whole fruit, allowing the children to comment if they would like to, encourage all the children to contribute where possible. After looking, smelling and feeling, ask the children to predict what the inside of a relatively unknown fruit or vegetable may look like, for example a pomegranate, dragon fruit, aubergine or fig. Many children are surprised when the inside is a contrasting colour or texture to the outside. An adult can act as scribe, recording their ideas on the flipchart, or more able children could be paired with a whiteboard and pen between them. Building on the literacy session in Week 2 the children's words can easily be translated into a simple list poem format, beginning 'Thank you for…' These are ideal to be read out in assembly or at a service to celebrate harvest. Each child could choose a fruit or vegetable, and give reasons for their thanks: Thank you for apples – they are crunchy and sweet. Thank you for peas – they are so good to eat! The list does not have to rhyme, however some children may be keen to supply a rhyming word!

If this is to be a guided activity…

…then work as a small group to ensure that all children are able to speak and be heard. Give each child a whiteboard. Pass around a fruit or vegetable for them to investigate, and ask them to quietly attempt to write something on their whiteboard to describe the fruit or vegetable. Encourage them to use a different sense each time. The adult can then read this out jointly with the child: Apples…*red and green*.

If this is to be an independent activity…

…then show the children where the basket of fruit and vegetables is and explain that they can smell, hold and look closely at these items over the week. Reiterate that they must not taste anything without an adult present. Provide sticky notes or word cards for the children to note down their responses. If you have a voice recorder then the children could talk to their friends, collecting responses to a single fruit or vegetable. Listen to these together and discuss.

To support, you may wish to identify one or two children during the whole-group activity at the outset, monitoring or recording their involvement and use of vocabulary when speaking and listening. The children can work together with an adult to explore a few fruits and vegetables in a small group. The adult can ask the children to talk to their neighbour (as a response partner) to ensure that all the children are able to rehearse speaking and listening. The children's descriptive words and phrases could be scribed by an adult onto an outline of the fruit or vegetable in question e.g. all the comments describing apples could be written together on a green apple shape. These make an attractive display. Encourage the children to help you to sound out the words needed to write each caption or phrase, segmenting orally and recognising the difference between a letter, a word and a phrase.

To extend the more able children, encourage them to write their own descriptive phrases to create a bank of ideas about each fruit or vegetable. Show them how to group their ideas together regarding the same fruit or vegetable as their friends, or extend them by asking them to write a sentence or caption for each of their five senses about a single fruit or vegetable. Give the children coloured sticky notes or strips of coloured card to help them to sort and order their descriptive responses. When they have written a phrase, show them how to re-read it to check for meaning, and then to read it to their friend (as a response partner) to see if they can help with any amendments or improve the choice of vocabulary.

Ideas for interactive display

Put out a selection of fruit and vegetables, either real or from the home corner. Provide some wicker baskets or role-play shopping baskets and tell the children that they are to sort the fruit and vegetables in any way they choose. The children could record their criteria on a sticky label. They could consider colour, size, texture, or where and how it grows, for example, on trees or underground.

At home, take your child with you when you are shopping for fruit and vegetables and let them choose something for themselves, or give them a picture of the fruit you want them to find. Look for similar fruit of different colours or unusually shaped fruit and vegetables to try.

Autumn food and harvest

Pumpkin soup

The children will be following a recipe to make soup using vegetables harvested in the autumn. They will measure, weigh and count as an introduction to capacity and weight.

Observation and assessment

Mathematics	Expected statements (ELGs for end of F2)
Shapes, space and measures	Children use everyday language to talk about size, weight, capacity, position, distance, time and money to compare quantities and objects and to solve problems. They recognise, create and describe patterns. They explore characteristics of everyday objects and shapes and use mathematical language to describe them.

Resources

* ⭐ Variety of vegetables harvested in the autumn, including pumpkin

* ⭐ Variety of tinned/packet soup made from different vegetables, with pictures on the packaging

* ⭐ Water to mix

* ⭐ Wooden spoon

* ⭐ Chopping board

* ⭐ Vegetable peelers

* ⭐ Suitable knives (select child-friendly vegetable knives if possible)

* ⭐ Saucepan

* ⭐ Hob

* ⭐ Bowls and spoons one for each child

Safety first!
Ensure that none of the children have allergies to any of the foods being investigated.

Storybooks

* ⭐ *Pumpkin Soup* by Helen Cooper

* ⭐ *Stone Soup* (traditional tale)

Key vocabulary

* names of vegetables selected

soup	cut	net
measure	chop	cylinder
weigh	slice	cuboid
time	pan	big
how much	ladle	bigger
how many	spoon	biggest
how long	bowl	small
cook	amount	smaller
boil	3D	smallest

What to do

Explain to the children that they are going to make soup from different vegetables and eat it together. Look together at the packaging from the shop-bought soup, ask: What vegetables are used in the different soups? How do the children know? Pass around the vegetables to be used, ensure that the children all know what they are called and can use their names correctly.

Read Pumpkin Soup and discuss the roles of the animals in the story. Have available a hob in an area separate to the children, for cooking the soup. Wash hands and demonstrate safely preparing the vegetables. Ensure that all the children are aware of the correct way to use a sharp knife, where appropriate. Encourage them to chop, peel, slice and cut vegetables and put them in the pan. Add water and boil on a stove until cooked, away from the children. You can choose to serve the soup either with chunks of recognisable vegetables in it, or blend it to a smooth consistency. Allow the children to eat some soup (serve with pieces of bread if you have reluctant vegetable eaters!) and discuss together which vegetables they could taste, smell or see. Finally, review the choices made – if they were to make soup again tomorrow, what would they do the same/differently? Are there any vegetables that they would not include, or are there some that they would like more of? Encourage them to go home and try to make vegetable soup with a family member.

If this is to be a guided activity…

…then the children can work in a very small group together with an adult to choose two or three vegetables they really like to make their own soup. Allow the children to be very hands-on with the preparation – many vegetables can be prepared by hand (see independent activity). In a small group children should be allowed to use vegetable peelers and knives safely and under supervision to learn the necessary skills. Each amount of chopped vegetable can be measured in a simple way (e.g. a cupful, or half a cup) or in a more accurate way using weighing scales and a simple recipe. An adult could act as scribe to record the ingredients on a flipchart or whiteboard. When the adult has cooked the soup then the children can sit together in a sociable manner and share a meal.

If this is to be an independent activity…

…then the preparation can be done by the children but of course the cooking part will be done by an adult. Show the children where the selection of vegetables is and explain that they can try this activity sometime this week, but that all children must wash their hands before going to this activity. Put out vegetables that can be prepared by hand (celery and green beans can be snapped into pieces; onion, once peeled and quartered, can be peeled into segments; mushrooms can be peeled or broken by hand, peas and broad beans can be shelled). Encourage them to choose their vegetable selection carefully and to record their choices on a whiteboard in the form of a simple pictorial recipe. Once they have put their chosen vegetables into the pan provided then an adult can cook the soup when convenient.

Ideas for interactive display

Provide the role-play equipment for cooking e.g. pans, wooden spoons, a ladle, bowls, plastic or wooden vegetables and, if possible, water. Encourage the children to choose three different vegetables and to make soup, using the water in the pan to stir and ladle out into the bowls. If there were little whiteboards available they could record the ingredients for their soup by drawing pictures.

Parents and carers as partners

At home, make some simple soups together from whatever you have in the cupboard – many vegetables make tasty soup. Alternatively, let them choose a soup when shopping and talk about the colour and texture of it when they are eating it at home. Can they taste the vegetables that are pictured on the packet?

Autumn food and harvest

Activity 3

Hedgehog bread rolls

The children will be making bread together, each shaping a ball of dough into a hedgehog shape complete with spines. They will recognise how different ingredients can combine to create something new, and understand how a recipe helps us to make food to eat.

Resources

Safety first!
Ensure that none of the children have allergies to any of the foods being investigated.

* White card

* White crêpe paper

* Simple bread recipe

* Ingredients as specified in recipe to make one small roll per child

* Olives/raisins and herbs such as rosemary stems to add eyes and spines

* Baking equipment as specified in recipe

* Weighing scales

* Clean children's scissors

* Aprons

* Oven

* Oven tray

* Sheet of baking parchment paper

Storybooks

* *The Little Red Hen* (traditional tale)

Observation and assessment

Understanding the world	Expected statements (ELGs)
The world	Children know about similarities and differences in relation to places, objects, materials and living things. They make observations of animals and plants and explain why some things occur, and talk about changes.
Technology	Children recognise that a range of technology is used in places such as homes and schools.

Key vocabulary

bread	olives	ball
dough	rise	point
yeast	knead	snip
flour	roll	spines
water	press	bake
herbs	shape	

What to do

Read the children the traditional tale of *The Little Red Hen*. Talk about the different ingredients needed to make bread and how it is baked. Explain that they are each going to make a small bread roll in the shape of a hedgehog, to eat afterwards. Provide chef's hats for each child made from a band of white card (the brim) and a circular piece of white crepe paper (the puffy bit in the centre) taped inside and explain that chefs wear hats to stop hair falling into the food.

Instruct them to wash their hands carefully before beginning. Show them the ingredients and the equipment, and ask the children how do we begin? Make a silly sequence of events, following exactly what the children instruct e.g. simply place the entire bag of flour, bag and all, into the bowl, and try to mix with a spoon. When the children laugh, say 'Oh! Well that's what you told me to do!' Keep on following their instructions in this way until they have put together a clear verbal structure for the bread making.

Discuss what a recipe is, and display an enlarged copy of a bread recipe preferably with some picture clues at each stage. Note that the language used is 'bossy' – the imperative is used (put/mix/stir) to begin each instruction. Demonstrate how to weigh carefully, explaining that the outcome will be altered if the quantities are incorrect. When the dough is ready to be shaped give a small ball to each child. Encourage them to shape it into a smooth hedgehog shape (a ball with a pointed nose) and then to use the clean scissors to carefully snip the dough to create spines. The mouth can also be cut this way. If you wish you can add more spines by poking the stems of rosemary into the hedgehog's back to stick up, and create eyes with olives or raisins. Have an oven available away from the children and bake the hedgehog rolls on an oven tray according to the recipe. If you put baking parchment on the tray before setting the rolls on it, you can write each child's name next to their own roll so that everyone eats their own!

If this is to be a guided activity…

…then the children can work together with an adult in small groups to bake the bread. It is possible to teach the initial part of the session to a large group as they are mostly sitting, listening and giving contributions. Then divide into smaller groups at the point where the ingredients are measured, mixed and kneaded into dough. Following the baking of the bread gather the children together again, firstly to look at the different hedgehog rolls, and then to sit together for the eating!

If this is to be an independent activity…

…it is not possible for the children to actually bake their own bread and eat it. However, they can easily simulate bread making and dough rolling using soft dough. If you are adventurous (and have an outdoor area and large aprons) you can put out flour, salt and water and let the children attempt to make their own dough. Give them a simple enlarged (and laminated) recipe sheet showing the quantities needed (using cupfuls) and let them experiment! This is a very messy activity if the children do this independently: if they add too much water it instantly becomes a sticky mess! Put the water into a slow pouring or sprinkling container to control the amount added at a time.

To support, work with only one or two children at a time, and let them be hands-on with each ingredient as it is added to the bowl. Let them run their fingers through the flour and the water, talking about how each one looks and feels before mixing to a dough. Let them press and knead, drawing their attention to the changes undergone by the ingredients. Model using the vocabulary and question the children carefully to see if they too can use the technical vocabulary particular to this task. Show them how to roll the dough into a ball and carefully snip the spines. If they are struggling to handle the dough, offer support throughout the week by having balls of soft dough on the malleable table for them to squeeze, press, roll and snip. Put out the baking equipment and the oven from the home corner to role-play making and preparing bread.

To extend, encourage the more able children to make some soft dough independently outside, using the simple recipe card. Tell them that they can add more ingredients to their plain soft dough to make it look, feel or smell different. Provide droppers with differently coloured food dye, droppers with mint, vanilla or lavender essence and beads, rice, beans or glitter to sprinkle in. Restrict the children to one of each type of ingredient to change the look, smell and feel of the dough. Encourage them to record their new recipe on a recipe card so that their friend can also make the same kind. Photograph the children holding their finished dough to put on the bottom of the recipe card, and collect these cards to make a recipe library for the other children to use.

Ideas for interactive display

Provide soft dough and a variety of different baking trays, pans and moulds. Show the children how to mould, twist, plait and roll the soft dough into different shapes before fitting it into the appropriate pan. If you also provide simple scales then the children can weigh similar sized balls of dough and experiment making different shaped 'loaves' to their friends.

At home, go to the bakery and look at all the different types and shapes of bread. Let the child choose a roll for their lunch. Bread is simple to make at home, and the child will be so proud if they make some bread for their family to eat!

Autumn food and harvest

Turnips and onions

The children will be exploring colour mixing to make different shades and tones of purple. Looking at natural shades in turnips and red onions, the children will be able to mix different colours and record these on a single painting.

Observation and assessment

Expressive arts and design	Expected statements (ELGs)
Exploring and using media and materials	They safely use and explore a variety of materials, tools and techniques, experimenting with colour, design, texture, form and function.
Being imaginative	Children use what they have learnt about media and materials in original ways, thinking about uses and purposes.

Key vocabulary

- mix
- stir
- paint
- brush
- palette
- shade
- tone
- light
- dark
- purple
- lilac
- violet
- red
- blue
- turnip
- red onion

Resources

- ★ Turnip
- ★ Red onion
- ★ Purple vegetables such as purple sprouting broccoli, aubergine, swede
- ★ Selection of purple paint colour charts (from DIY store)
- ★ Ready mixed 'squeezy' paint or powder paint in red, blue and white
- ★ White sugar paper at least A3
- ★ Brushes (one each)
- ★ Paper towel
- ★ Water pots (one each)
- ★ Mixing palette with at least four spaces (one each)

Storybooks

- ★ *The Enormous Turnip* (traditional tale)
- ★ *Mr Wolf and the Enormous Turnip* by Jan Fearnley
- ★ *Mouse Paint* by Ellen Stoll Walsh

What to do

Explain to the children that they are going to mix some paints to make the colour purple. Teach the children that the primary colours of red, yellow and blue cannot be made from any other colours. This is why they are called primary colours. The colours of purple, orange and green are called secondary colours and they are made by mixing two primary colours together. Show the children the turnip and the red onion, and any other purple vegetables you can find (purple sprouting broccoli, aubergine, swede etc.). Discuss with the children what colour they are, and note that although they are all called purple they are not exactly the same colour.

Cut a red onion in half and look at the pattern the segments make inside. Demonstrate colour mixing to the children. Show them how to put a little red paint into the palette, clean their brush in the water and on the paper towel and dip just the tip of their brush into the blue paint to pick up a little colour to mix into the palette. Draw a large onion shape on the A3 paper with segments showing as if it is cut in half. Show how the red colour has changed just a little, and then use the paint to fill in one section of the red onion on the A3 paper. Repeat – pick up a little blue paint on the brush, mix it in the same palette with the existing paint and look at the subtle change again. Paint the neighbouring segment to the first, showing the children the change in colour. Repeat several times until the onion segments are all painted. If the children are making really dark shades of purple which do not change colour, let them add some white to their palette or to begin again with red in a clean section of the palette. When the onion paintings are dry, cut them out and tape a bundle of white string to the bottom in the style of roots. These look great displayed in a row on a wall of black paper, as if they are growing in the ground.

If this is to be a guided activity…

…then work as a group to make different shades of purple paint. The children on one table could pass their palette to their neighbour to share their paint colour. Try to encourage the children to paint each section of the onion in turn so that the effect is of a steadily changing colour chart.

If this is to be an independent activity…

…then put out the red, blue and white paint on a table and let the children experiment with colour mixing to create many different shades and tones of purple. Make a purple craft table – provide purple crayons, chalks, felt tips, pencils, purple paper, card, foil and Clingfilm for the children to create their own artwork.

To support or extend

To support, the children can work together with an adult to look at shades and tones of purple, violet and lilac around the environment. Take a digital camera on a walk around the setting and photograph items found. Make a purple collection – lay a large sheet of purple paper or a purple cloth on the floor and encourage the children to collect objects that are purple to display together. Let them sort the objects according to their own criteria – they may sort by colour, texture, shape, size or type of object. Encourage them to explain their choices to the group. Use the purple objects to make a representational picture of something important to them.

To extend the more able children, encourage them to work independently to create a shade of purple by colour mixing. Have available individual paint sample charts and strips from DIY stores that show graduated changes in shade and tone, light to dark and let the children use these to match their own paint. Let them cut out a patch from their paint and a patch from the colour chart to make a matching pair. With a collection of squares cut out from the purple paint charts encourage the children to sort or group the squares into a colour chart of their own devising, perhaps from light to dark tones, or warm and cool colours. Give reasons for their choices. Extend this further by making a purple mosaic picture from the assorted squares.

Ideas for interactive display

Create a colour table by inviting the children to collect together, or bring from home, a selection of objects which are all shades and tones of purple. Make some labels of colour words such as lilac, violet and indigo. If possible, construct a washing line so the children can peg the objects onto the line in order from light purple to dark purple. The colour strips available at DIY stores showing different shades of paint are extremely useful for demonstrating to the children how many different degrees of purple there are. They can also use these to find the matching shade to their object.

Parents and carers as partners

At home, make a collection of purple objects. Put them all together and talk about the different shades and tones you can see. Take your child to the fruit and vegetable shop: can they find three purple foods?

Autumn leaves and colour  Activity 1

What's in the feely box?

The children will be describing natural autumnal objects to a partner after choosing them from a feely box, using their senses and a range of vocabulary.

Resources

★ A 'feely box' that the children can put their hands inside but are not able to see the objects inside

★ Pairs of natural autumn objects: pine cones, conkers, conker shells, green leaves, dry leaves, twigs, stones, autumn fruits such as an apple or berries, or anything else you would find at this time of year

Storybooks

★ *A Golden Leaf: The Story of Autumn* by Rosie McCormick

★ *Ferdie and the Falling Leaves* by Julia Rawlinson

Key vocabulary

• feel	• cold
• touch	• heavy
• rough	• light
• smooth	• dry
• hard	• damp
• soft	• crackly
• bumpy	• spiky
• prickly	• (other adjectives related to how an object feels to touch)
• furry	

Observation and assessment

Communication and Language	Expected statements (ELGs)
Listening and attention	Children listen attentively in a range of situations. They give their attention to what others say and respond appropriately, while engaged in another activity.
Speaking	Children express themselves effectively, showing awareness of listeners' needs. They use past, present and future forms accurately when talking about events that have happened or are to happen in the future. They develop their own narratives and explanations by connecting ideas or events.

What to do

Show the children the selection of objects that will be inside the feely box. Let them pass each one around the circle so that they can experience touching them. Tell the children that there are two of each item, and that they are going to match the objects with their partner. Practise this on the carpet, using the sense of sight as well as touch. Line up the paired objects. Introduce the feely box to the children; show them how they can put their hands inside through the holes but that they cannot see inside it.

Put one of each item into the box and close the lid. Demonstrate putting your own hands through the holes and selecting an object to hold. Then model saying an adjective to describe the object you are holding. Ask a child to come to the objects in the middle of the group and place to one side the object/s they think you might be holding inside the box e.g. if you said 'spiky' the child could select the conker shell, pinecone and twig. Use the key vocabulary where relevant, repeating and rephrasing the child's answer to include the correct adjectives. There are two levels at which this activity could then continue: you could provide some more information about the object you are holding inside the box in order for the child to discard any objects which do not have the characteristics you are describing, or they could look at the possible objects and ask you a question to try to narrow down the options until there is only one object left. This activity supports the use of a key in Science and ICT later in Key Stage 1.

If this is to be a guided activity…

…then the children can work together in a small group with an adult supervising the turn taking and modelling the use of the correct vocabulary. Children often find it hard to ask a question which narrows down a field without actually saying, 'Is it the pine cone?' They may need many attempts where they are the selector and the adult asks the questions using adjectives before they are able to play this game successfully.

If this is to be an independent activity…

…then show the children where the collection of objects will be, and explain that sometime during the week they can play this activity with a friend. If they are finding it difficult to phrase and answer the questions correctly then put two of each object in the feely box and let them take it in turns to select the first object and take it out of the box. Let the partner use all of their senses to investigate the visible object before putting their hand into the feely box and trying to select the matching object by touch alone.

To support or extend

To support, narrow the field of objects to only one or two that are very distinctive, for example a pine cone, a large flat pebble and a feather. Let the children look at and handle each of the objects, modelling the language to describe what they are holding. Play simple games with objects that are visible in front of them: Please choose something that is heavy/spiky/smooth moving onto asking a question that could be applicable to two of the objects so that the children have to distinguish between them. When this has been modelled many times by the adult, encourage the child to ask a question of their own.

To extend the more able children, encourage them to play the game with their peers. Introduce more objects which have similar characteristics. Let the children go outdoors to choose their own natural objects, and on return indoors involve them in deciding which objects are to go in the feely box. They should use detailed vocabulary, a greater range of adjectives and justify their choices to the other children.

Ideas for interactive display

Provide two blindfolds and a selection of differently textured objects in pairs. Encourage the children to work with a friend to match the objects together. Each child wears a blindfold, selects an object from the table and describes it to their partner. If they think they are describing the same item they remove their blindfold to check. Leave room on the display table for children to add items of their own which they believe have a distinctive texture.

Parents and carers as partners

At home, encourage your child to play games such as *Guess Who?* and *Happy Families*. The game of *I Spy* can also be altered to include adjectives: I spy, with my little eye, something that is… spiky! These games all require skills of close observation, good listening and the need to ask clear, accurate questions.

Autumn leaves and colour

Leaves on the line!

The children will be ordering numbered leaves on a washing line and choosing different numbers to make simple number bonds to ten and number sentences.

Observation and assessment

Mathematics	Expected statements (ELGs)
Numbers	Children count reliably with numbers from 1 to 20, place them in order and say which number is one more or one less than a given number. Using quantities and objects, they add and subtract two single-digit numbers and count on or back to find the answer. They solve problems, including doubling, halving and sharing.

Resources

★ Coloured outlines of leaf shapes each clearly numbered 0–20

★ Number card 10

★ Washing line securely fixed at child height, indoors or outdoors

★ Clothes pegs that have a broad grip and can be used by small hands

★ Individual whiteboards and pens for recording

★ Mathematical symbols cards + and =

★ Bead strings fixed at either end, with ten beads on

★ Counting apparatus

Storybooks

★ *Leaf Trouble* by Jonathan Emmett

★ *Leaves Fall Down: Learning about autumn leaves* by Lisa Bullard

Key vocabulary

- number names 0-20
- more
- less
- one more
- altogether
- how many now?
- next

- after
- before
- add
- addition
- subtract
- total
- equals

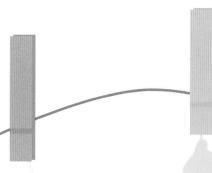

What to do

Explain to the children that they are going to do some counting, ordering and sorting, and that the leaves on the washing line are going to help them to do this. Show them a basket with a pile of numbered leaf shapes, 0–10 to begin with. Explain that the leaves all blew down and that now we need to put them onto the washing line in the correct order, using the pegs. Select 11 children to each choose a leaf from the basket. Ask them to stand in a line and ask the other children if the leaves are in the correct places to make the numbers count in order. Select children one at a time to either come out to the line to move a child and leaf to a new place, or if they are able they could give an instruction without physically moving e.g. 'Evie, swap places with Jamilla'. Continue until the leaves are in order. Take them from the children and peg them onto the washing line in order. This activity can be repeated with numbers 11–20 if necessary. Demonstrate counting along the line, pointing to each leaf in turn. Encourage the children to join in with the counting. Begin the counting at different places along the line, don't always begin at zero or one. Explain to the children that they are going to divide the line of leaves into two groups, to make a simple addition to ten (or 20, if you are extending the learning).

NB Don't forget to remove zero from the line or you will get an inaccurate result!

Slide the leaves apart, to make two groups of five with a space in the middle. What can the children tell you about what they can see? Look for answers using number names and mathematical terms like 'equals' or 'the same as'. Ensure that the children understand that although you have physically moved the leaves you have not taken any away: the total is still the same. Recount if necessary. Read the number sentence out loud: 'Five and five equals ten'. Show the children the + and = symbol cards, explain their meaning. Peg these on to the washing line, re-read the number sentence and peg the number card 10 at the end of the line. Explain to the children that there are ten leaves on the line today, so the number card at the end of the number sentence will stay as 10. Repeat the division into two groups, sliding the leaves along the washing line to make different number bonds to ten. Keep on talking out loud and saying the number sentence many times to embed the concept in the children's minds.

If this is to be a guided activity...

...then the children can work together with an adult to make their own number bonds to ten. They could begin with something fixed, such as ten beads on a string, and practise making different groups but always counting along to ten. They could pictorially record their beads on the string, and write the numbers and the symbols underneath.

If this is to be an independent activity...

...then explain to the children that they are to use either a ten bead string or ten cubes of the same colour to create two groups which have ten in total. If they are grouping ten loose objects it may help to have two small containers for them to put their objects into, or they may lose one on the floor and all their number sentences will only add up to nine! Encourage them to record with both pictures and a correct number sentence.

To support or extend

To support, give the children only five cubes, repeating the activity above but with lower numbers. Use a hungry puppet with an opening mouth, and place a cube on each of the child's fingers. Ask them to hold up their hand and count the cubes together. When the child closes their eyes the hungry puppet 'eats' one of the cubes. Talk with the child about how many are gone, and how many are left. Use the words 'one and four/four and one' many times in the discussion so that the child begins to understand the number bond. Finally check the puppet's mouth, retrieve the eaten cube, replace it on the finger and count to five again. Repeat and repeat!

To extend the more able children, encourage them to work with larger numbers up to 20, looking for patterns they know from their number bonds to ten. To record, ask the children to use squared paper and two differently coloured crayons. Begin to colour in the correct number of cubes to make a number sentence, recording accurately with numbers and symbols underneath.

Ideas for interactive display

Have lots of groups of ten items, e.g. beads, cubes, buttons, pegs, pencils, small world animals, cars or trains. Using number cards 0–10 encourage the children to count out ten of the items into two groups (two laminated large hand shapes work well as placemats) and put a matching number card on each. They could record these ideas onto small whiteboards or take photographs of their findings. If there is room on the display for a washing line they could also peg items up in two groups. If the display area is outside do not be afraid to use large items to count with e.g. car tyres, milk crates or bikes, as children love to work on a large scale. They could chalk their numbers onto the floor in the beginning of a number sentence.

Parents and carers as partners

At home, encourage children to count, sort, order and match quantities of different things (e.g. buttons, matchsticks, pasta shapes) and make a number card to go with it. Play lots of games with dice and cards, moving on a counter, climbing up a ladder or sliding down a snake are all excellent for number practice.

Autumn leaves and colour

Activity 3

What shall we wear on a windy walk?

The children will be looking at different clothes worn by their friends on different occasions, and talking about why they are similar or different. The children will then choose which clothes would be suitable for a windy walk in autumn, giving reasons for their choices.

Observation and assessment

Understanding the world	Expected statements (ELGs)
People and communities	Children talk about past and present events in their own lives and in the lives of family members. They know that other children don't always enjoy the same things, and are sensitive to this. They know about similarities and differences between themselves and others, and among families, communities and traditions.

Key vocabulary

- wear
- wore
- warm
- cold
- thick
- thin

- waterproof
- names of different items of clothing
- terms to describe different weather, temperature
- colour names

Resources

★ Photographs of people wearing different clothes at different times of the year, to show on the whiteboard

★ Children's own seasonal photographs

★ Selection of seasonal clothing items: woollen hat and mittens, swimsuit, sunhat, wellington boots, raincoat and umbrella; T-shirt and shorts; trousers, sweater, sundress

★ Clothing catalogues

Storybooks

★ *Warm Clothes (Preparing for Winter)* by Gail Saunders-Smith

★ *The Man Who Wore All His Clothes* by Allan Ahlberg

★ *Lulu's Clothes* by Camilla Reid

What to do

Show the children a photograph on the whiteboard or a poster of someone wearing warm clothes, hats and mittens, playing in the snow. Ask the children about their experiences of playing in the snow (there may be children who have not yet experienced snow in the UK). What did they wear? Invite children to bring in their own photographs showing themselves playing outside in a type of weather, e.g. snow, sunshine on the beach and ask them to share their photographs with the group. What is the same about the clothing they all wear in the snow? What is different?

Show the children the selection of clothing, and ask a child to select from the assortment anything which would be useful on a snowy day. Encourage them to give reasons for their choices. Select some more clothing from the collection and hold it up (choose things that you would wear on a sunny beach, e.g. swimsuit, sunhat). Ask the children who have a photograph of themselves wearing similar clothing to stand up with their photograph. Discuss as a group the similarities between each photograph. Explain why the clothing worn on a sunny beach is different from that worn on a snowy day: what properties do the clothes need to have for each weather condition? Demonstrate sorting the selected clothing into piles for different types of weather discussed so far. Encourage them to use the key vocabulary and to give reasons for their choices.

Explain to the children that they are to think of the type of clothing that would be necessary for an autumn walk through the woods, on a windy day. Ask them to justify their choices, talking about the properties of each material or item, e.g. 'Wellies because it might be muddy and they will keep the mud out' or 'I wouldn't wear just a T-shirt because the wind would make my arms cold.'

If this is to be a guided activity…

…then the children can work together with an adult to sort the clothing into piles on the carpet suitable for different occasions. Encourage the children to write labels on individual whiteboards to name the piles, either types of weather or the names of the seasons. Discuss with the children the possibility of the same item of clothing being worn at different times of year – have any of the children worn their wellingtons on a sunny beach when they were paddling in the cold sea, as well as on a rainy day or in the snow? What is it about wellingtons that makes them suitable for different occasions? (Waterproofness.)

If this is to be an independent activity…

…then show the children where the basket of clothing is and explain that they can try this activity sometime this week. Show them the catalogues with pictures of clothing and explain that these are pictures for cutting out – they are not books for reading and that no one wants them anymore. Give the children some large coloured pieces of paper for sticking their clothing items onto – colour code the paper for each season, e.g. white for winter, orange for autumn, green for spring and yellow for summer. Let the children make a collection of suitable clothing for each season and predominant weather type. They could draw other details to the large collages to make it typical of the weather – beach items to summer, a flying kite and falling leaves to the autumn scene.

To support or extend

To support, give the children a suitcase containing clothing suitable for only two occasions, for example to wear outdoors (coat, hat, shoes etc.) or to wear to bed (pyjamas, dressing gown, slippers). In a small group, allow the children to take turns to select an item of clothing and place it in a hoop on the floor. Encourage them to give a reason for their choice. The children may initially group the items by colour or gender – this is fine, as long as they are giving suitable reasons for their choices. When the children have sorted and grouped the clothing in a certain way ask them to think if there are other ways of sorting the clothing (e.g. by material, size, colour), before drawing their attention to the properties of the clothing and when it would be necessary to wear it. Finally, encourage the children to talk about their own special or significant clothing and why it is special to them.

To extend the more able children show them a suitcase filled with different types, styles and sizes of clothing. Encourage them to select their own criteria for sorting and grouping the clothing into sets. This activity will promote lots of discussion, reasoning and justification for their choices. Ensure that the children understand that other children's choices are valid, and that they must work together to achieve the outcome. Include in the suitcase clothes which belonged to a baby, a toddler and an adult, discussing with the children the clothing they wore when they were a baby and how it is different from what they wear now. If possible, include clothing which is special (e.g. a jewelled, sequined party dress, or a Christening gown), old and worn (e.g. a holey old sock) and from a different culture to most of the children. Help the children to appreciate that what is special or significant to them may not be to another child, and vice versa.

Ideas for interactive display

Display a selection of pictures and photographs of children wearing different types of clothing, alongside photographs of different types of weather and temperatures. Encourage the children to link the pictures into matching pairs with string. Staple one of the ends of pieces of string to the photographs of children, leaving them dangling free. The children can take the free end of a piece of string, consider the picture it is already attached to and use Blu-tack to join it to a partner picture.

Parents and carers as partners

At home, let the children cut up pictures of people in old catalogues and magazines. They can group the clothing into that which is required for different types of weather. This will require skills of observation, fine motor skills such as cutting, thought and reasoning when grouping the sets.

Autumn leaves and colour

Patterned orange leaves

The children will be mixing red and yellow paint to make orange, and painting large leaf shapes looking at shades, tones and pattern.

Observation and assessment

Expressive arts and design	Expected statements (ELGs)
Exploring and using media and materials	They safely use and explore a variety of materials, tools and techniques, experimenting with colour, design, texture, form and function.
Being imaginative	Children use what they have learnt about media and materials in original ways, thinking about uses and purposes.

Key vocabulary

• mix	• light	• pattern
• stir	• dark	• lines
• paint	• red	• spots
• brush	• yellow	• dots
• palette	• orange	• zig zag
• shade	• gold	
• tone	• leaf	

Resources

★ Collection of coloured autumnal leaves

★ Selection of red, orange and yellow paint colour charts (from DIY store)

★ Ready-mixed 'squeezy' paint or powder paint in red and yellow

★ Gold paint

★ White sugar paper A3 size

★ Paper towel

★ Paintbrushes (one each)

★ Water pot (one each)

★ Mixing palette with at least four spaces (one each)

Story books

★ *Leaf Man* and *Red Leaf, Yellow Leaf* by Lois Ehlert

★ *Why do leaves change colour?* by Betsy Maestro

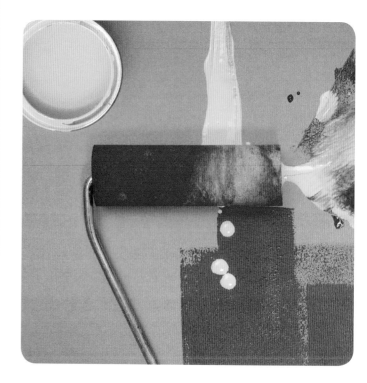

What to do

Remind the children of the secondary colour mixing that they did in Week 3, making shades of purple. Explain that this time they are going to use yellow and red paint to make shades and tones of orange, and to use gold to decorate with patterns. Show them a collection of autumn leaves, letting them choose one each to look at closely. Talk about the many colours they can see, and let them take their leaf around to those held by their peers trying to find a colour match.

Provide colour charts as individual strips from DIY stores that show graduated changes in shade and tone, light to dark and introduce the key vocabulary along with the colour charts. Give each child a colour strip close to the predominant colour of their leaf and ask them to compare the light to dark shades on their strip with the colours on their leaf, searching for an exact match. Allow the children to group their leaves on the carpet into hoops: mostly red, mostly orange, mostly yellow and so on. Take one of the groups and ask the children to help you make a 'colour strip' from the leaves, ordering them from light to dark.

Explain that they are going to paint a leaf shape with many different shades and tones of orange paint. Show the children the A3 paper and draw a large leaf shape on it. Mix a little red paint into some yellow paint in order to make it slightly darker. Give each child a strip of paper for them to record a sample of the colour they have created before they paint some onto their leaf shape. This activity is an extension of the red onion colour mixing from Week 3; this time there are no specific parts of the leaf shape to paint but they are to decide for themselves how to fill their leaf with different shades and tones of orange. Demonstrate different patterns: squares; lines; blocks; around the edge of the shape in a concentric pattern or their own design. Ensure that the children understand that they should always begin with the yellow paint (as it is lighter) and to add a tiny amount of the darker red each time, slowly changing the colour. When the leaf is full of colour and no background paper colour remains, it is finished. When it's dry the children can decorate it further using a thin brush and gold paint. These large leaves look particularly effective displayed all together at the top of a corrugated cardboard 'tree trunk', particularly if the leaves are able to 'grow' onto the ceiling.

If this is to be a guided activity…

…then the children can work together with an adult to carefully mix the red and yellow paint to make orange. The adult should model the key vocabulary and encourage the children to change the colour as subtly as possible by only adding a small amount of red paint each time. Let the children share their shades of orange with each other if they have made one they particularly like.

If this is to be an independent activity…

…then show the children an 'orange' craft table, stocked with many different types of paper, card, tissue, cellophane and fabric in different oranges. Provide strips of card and ask the children to make a collage colour chart, choosing different shades and tones of orange and asking them to display them from light to dark along the strip. Put examples of the paint charts from DIY stores on the table to guide them.

To support or extend

To support, help the children to look through old magazines and catalogues to find shades of orange. Encourage them to cut out each example and place it on a large piece of paper. With guidance they can begin to move the orange pieces around, beginning to make a colour chart of shades and tones of orange. Use the DIY colour charts to indicate to the children how subtle colour changes can be. When they are satisfied that they have a graduated colour chart they can glue the pieces of orange down in a line.

To extend the more able children, encourage them to work independently to use red and yellow cellophane, tissue paper and crêpe paper to make orange. Show them how to overlap the red and yellow cellophane and look through it: does it make orange? Investigate tissue paper: how do the colours change when they overlap? Does this change when it's wet? Explore the colour transfer from crêpe paper when it's wet: how can the children use this to make orange? These water activities can be quite messy – they are probably more suitable for outside!

Ideas for interactive display

Create a collection of orange tissue papers and cellophanes. Encourage the children to look through them and comment upon what they observe, and how the different shades of orange change the appearance of existing objects. By including yellow and orange cellophane the children can also begin to mix colours.

Parents and carers as partners

At home let the children make a collection of familiar orange objects e.g. toys, crayons, fruit, clothing and household objects. Help them to group them into a colour chart from light to dark. This will enable them to differentiate between colours and experiment with textures.

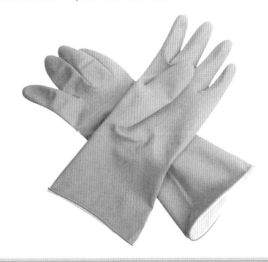

Autumn festivals and light  Activity 1

The story of Rama and Sita

The children will be sharing the book of the story of Rama and Sita and reading together, making masks and role-playing the story independently.

Resources

- ★ A version of the story of Rama and Sita with clear pictures

- ★ Some brightly coloured scarves with sequins and beads

- ★ Pictures of the main characters in the story to make into masks (print from the internet)

- ★ Elastic or lolly sticks

- ★ Stapler

- ★ Sellotape

Storybooks

- ★ *The Divali Story* by Anita Ganeri (available as a big book and a small version)

- ★ *Rama and the Demon King* by Jessica Souhami (dual language versions are available)

Key vocabulary

- Rama
- Sita
- Lakshman
- Hanuman (the monkey king)
- Lanka (the island)
- Divali/festival/light

Observation and assessment

Communication and Language	Expected statements (ELGs)
Understanding	They answer 'how' and 'why' questions about their experiences and in response to stories or events.
Speaking	They develop their own narratives and explanations by connecting ideas or events.

Literacy	Expected statements (ELGs)
Reading	Children read and understand simple sentences. They use phonic knowledge to decode regular words and read them aloud accurately. They demonstrate understanding when talking with others about what they have read, or what has been read to them.

Expressive arts and design	Expected statements (ELGs)
Being imaginative	They represent their own ideas, thoughts and feelings through design and technology, art, music, dance, role-play and stories.

What to do

Set up the book where all the children can clearly see the pictures and share the story together, looking at the illustrations to help the children appreciate the characters and culture of the setting. Discuss the festival of Divali, explain to the children that this is sometimes called the festival of light and explain why the lights are important. Use the key vocabulary where relevant, letting the children practise saying words which are new to them. Explain that in the country where the story is set people speak a different language to English, and that many of the people to whom the story is important also speak a variety of languages. Encourage any bilingual children in the setting to share words they know in their home language. Show the children the dual language text if you have one, and talk about the similarities and differences between their language and written English.

Look at the character pictures you have printed from the internet and demonstrate how to use them to make a mask. Show the children how to attach the lolly stick to the back of the pictures so the mask can be held in front of the face or attach elastic to wear it around the head. Talk about the colours and clothes worn by the people in the story – refer back to the book together to look at how they were worn. Let the children look at and hold the scarves before draping and wrapping each other to make 'clothes'.

If this is to be a guided activity…

…then the children can work together with an adult to retell the story, with the adult acting as narrator and reading from the book. The children can take it in turns to wear the mask of each character, and behave according to the spoken word of the narrating adult.

If this is to be an independent activity…

…then show the children where the collection of scarves, storybook, and mask-making equipment will be, and explain that sometime during the week they are to choose from the basket with a friend in order to act out the story. Show the children how to make the masks, and let them play at being different characters.

To support or extend

To support, work in a small group with the children, reading the story and looking closely at the book together. Make observations and share comments with the children, explaining in simple terms what is happening to each character and asking the children to predict what might happen next. Encourage the children to choose their favourite character mask and 'become' the character to act out a short part of the story. If the children find it difficult to do this, model it for them by dressing in a mask and scarf and 'hot-seating' the character, letting the children talk to you and ask questions.

To extend the more able children, encourage them to become one of the characters in the story. Show them what 'hot seating' is (putting yourself into the character's place in order to answer questions or flesh out the character more) and let them take it in turns to either be in the hot seat or to ask questions of the character in the hot seat. Give them further books with traditional tales from a mixture of cultures and allow them to explore the stories through drama and dressing up, letting them create their own characters and extend existing characters through their imagination.

Ideas for interactive display

Put out laminated pictures showing key scenes and characters from the story of Rama and Sita. Let the children play, sort and order them when they are telling the story. Provide lolly sticks and white sticky labels for the children to make little character puppets to use in their retelling. If possible have an audio or digital version of the story for the children to act along to.

Parents and carers as partners

At home, make a dressing up box containing a hat, a tie, a fancy scarf or a mask. Let the children invent a character, and make up some adventures. The character could be based upon a well known character from a book at first, in order that your child can simply re-enact the story.

Autumn festivals and light  Activity 2

Make 3D shaped fireworks

The children will be choosing appropriate 3D shapes to construct models of fireworks such as rockets and Catherine wheels.

Observation and assessment

Mathematics	Expected statements (ELGs)
Space, shape and measures	Children use everyday language to talk about size, weight, capacity, position, distance time and money to compare quantities and objects and to solve problems. They recognise, create and describe patterns. They explore characteristics of everyday objects and shapes and use mathematical language to describe them.

Resources

★ Pictures of fireworks, including rockets and Catherine wheels

★ 3D wooden shapes

★ Assorted boxes

★ Masking tape

★ Coloured card and 2D shapes

Storybooks

★ *Hovis the Hedgehog: Bonfire Night* by Lynda Leigh-Crawford

★ *Bonfire Night: Don't Forget* by Monica Hughes

★ *Bonfire Night (Holidays and Festivals)* by Nancy Dickmann

Key vocabulary

- bonfire
- firework
- flame
- spark
- rocket
- Catherine wheel
- 3D shape
- cylinder
- pyramid
- tube
- cone
- round
- roll
- spin
- turn

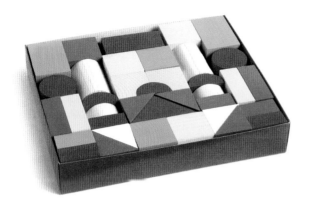

What to do

Explain to the children that they are going to make some fireworks from box modelling. Show them some pictures of fireworks, beginning with a simple rocket. Can they name any of the shapes they are made from? Using the tray of 3D wooden shapes, invite a child to select some shapes to 'build' a rocket, for example by placing a cone on the top of a cylinder. Frequently use the key vocabulary, repeating the 3D shape names to consolidate the vocabulary for the children. Encourage the children to first design their firework from the wooden 3D shapes before choosing similar shaped boxes from the collection. Cone-shaped boxes are difficult to find so it might be advisable to use some coloured card to make some different shapes and sized cones to add to the collection of boxes.

Now provide the junk modelling materials for the children to construct their own fireworks. Demonstrate by choosing suitable shapes from the collection of boxes, speaking aloud to justify each choice, discarding boxes that are too big, or which are the wrong shape. Use the masking tape as a simple and quick method of joining the boxes as there is no drying time, it's easy for the children to cut or tear it and it can be painted over.

As a supporting activity, put out different construction toys each day so that the children can investigate making rocket shapes from Lego, Sticklebricks, connecting straws and other types of joining construction.

If this is to be a guided activity…

…then the children can work together with an adult to make a box model firework of their choice. Help them to use masking tape to join their model together, and check that the children can use the correct vocabulary and names for the 3D shapes. Show the children how a 2D card circle can quickly be changed into a cone, and let them experiment with differently-sized circles. Help the children to make sticky name labels for the different 3D shapes in their firework model.

If this is to be an independent activity…

then show the children where the box of resources will be, and explain that they can try this activity sometime during the week. Put up some pictures of fireworks, along with labels to name the different types of 3D shapes. If you have lots of boxes they could be separated into differently labelled baskets to help the children find what they are searching for. Encourage them to make their own firework model from the boxes. Put out some sticky labels for the children to label each type of 3D shape in their firework model.

To support or extend

To support, let a small group of children first sort out the box of wooden 3D shapes into those which roll and those which don't. Explain that the rocket body needs to be a cylinder. Give the children a long cardboard tube, for example from the inside of a wrapping paper roll and let them decide how long they want the rocket body to be. The adult could cut to length for the children. Can they find any other shapes around the classroom that are also cylinders? (e.g. pens, glue sticks). Show the children how a cone can be made from a 2D card circle, and talk about other cone shapes that the children are familiar with (e.g. ice cream cones, witches hats, road traffic cones etc.). Help the children to join and decorate their box model.

To extend the more able children, provide them with some 2D nets of simple shapes and show them how to fold them into 3D shapes and tape them together with masking tape. They could also explore some moving pictures. Make a moving picture from a piece of A4 card for the background and some simple rocket shapes and Catherine wheels (circles). Show the children how to attach the shapes to the background using split pins so that the shapes can move or turn. The rockets could be attached to a drinking straw and poked through a slit in the card background so that they can be 'flown' up into the sky. Encourage them to think about the placing and positioning of the shapes on their picture so that all their items fit on.

Ideas for interactive display

Put out the wooden shapes for the children to build with. Encourage them to take a photograph of their model and then display the photograph on the table for other children to copy. If any improvements or alterations are made ask the children to record these by photograph or by drawing on a clipboard. Support all children when playing to use the correct mathematical vocabulary.

Parents and carers as partners

At home, collect any old boxes and cartons for the children to make models and structures with. They can be on a small scale (e.g. fit onto a table top) or a much larger scale (e.g. use several fruit boxes to make a train or a castle outside!) Don't worry too much about decorating them – your child will have a much better imagination than you and won't need detail to make it 'real'!

Autumn festivals and light

Lighting a lamp

The children will be making models of diva lights from clay, and understanding the significance of light to those people who celebrate Divali.

Observation and assessment

Understanding the world	Expected statements (ELGs)
People and communities	They know about similarities and differences between themselves and others, and among families, communities and traditions.

Key vocabulary

- clay
- dough
- roll
- press
- sausage
- cylinder
- circle
- spiral
- coil
- light
- lamp
- candle
- flame
- tea light

Resources

★ Clay

★ Salt dough or soft dough

★ Tea light candles

★ Paint and sequins

★ Video clip of the Divali festival celebrations (search on the internet)

Storybooks

★ *Lighting a Lamp: A Divali Story* by Jonny Zucker

★ *Rama and the Demon King* by Jessica Souhami (dual language versions are available)

Safety first!
This diva is purely for decoration and a real candle flame should not be lit inside it as it is not fire retardant.

What to do

Share the story of Divali with the children, discussing the significance of the lights and lamps to people who celebrate this festival. Explain why it is sometimes called the festival of light, and demonstrate this to the children by showing them some film clips of people celebrating Divali (in Leicester, for example, more than 35,000 people attended the switch on of the lights in 2011; it is thought to be the biggest celebration outside India). During Divali the Goddess Lakshmi is believed to visit homes that are well lit, so families decorate their homes with many lights and candles. Show the children a picture of diva, and explain that they are going to make a model in the form of a simple decorated coil pot big enough to fit a tea light candle inside.

Demonstrate with the soft dough or salt dough practising the techniques of rolling, moulding and coiling a pot. Show the children how to roll out a sausage shape on the board using both hands. Intentionally roll it too far so that it becomes spindly and breaks to highlight the importance of keeping the cylinder shaped sausage approximately the same shape along its length. Show the children how to cut around an upturned cup to make a circular base, and then to coil the sausage shape around the base creating the walls of the pot. Make as many sausage shapes as necessary until the pot is tall enough – keep testing the design of the pot by putting the tea light candle inside, to check for suitability.

To decorate the diva use different everyday objects (e.g. Lego, pencils, forks) to press into the soft clay or dough, making an imprint. When complete place the tea lights inside the divas, just for decoration.

Tell the children that this activity can be undertaken independently with soft dough, but that to create the diva from clay and decorate it with paint and sequins an adult will be needed to support.

If this is to be a guided activity…

…then the children can work together with an adult to explore the properties of the clay. Let the children investigate rolling, pressing, kneading and marking the clay with different objects before making their diva. When the clay is dry (or fired, depending on the type you use) the divas can be painted a metallic colour such as gold, or a bright colour, and then 'varnished' with PVA. Press sequins into the glue as it is drying to create a shiny finish.

If this is to be an independent activity…

…then explain that the malleable table will contain soft dough and all the items required to make a diva independently. Put laminated pictures of different styles of diva on the table so that the children can investigate using different objects to make the imprinted patterns.

If the children wish to keep the diva they made, it can be baked in the oven on a medium heat until it is hardened, and then painted or varnished with PVA glue.

To support or extend

To support, give the children a simple small sphere of clay and show them how to press it down with their hands to make a roughly circular base. Show them how to roll a sausage shape from a ball using both hands – if their sausage is changing diameter randomly keep re-rolling it into a sausage for them. Help them to coil the sausage around the circular base. Repeat once or twice until a shallow diva has been made. Give them a pencil or the end of a paintbrush to poke into the soft clay to make a simple pattern. Explain that this is a place to put a special candle – discuss when they have seen candles used and their special significance (perhaps for birthdays or other celebrations).

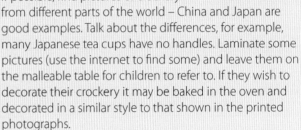

To extend the more able children by encouraging them to look at the design of other plates, bowls and cups and to try to model these from soft dough in a similar fashion. If possible, find pictures of crockery from different parts of the world – China and Japan are good examples. Talk about the differences, for example, many Japanese tea cups have no handles. Laminate some pictures (use the internet to find some) and leave them on the malleable table for children to refer to. If they wish to decorate their crockery it may be baked in the oven and decorated in a similar style to that shown in the printed photographs.

Ideas for interactive display

Display pictures and artefacts from the Hindu tradition. If you have children of Hindu faith in the setting invite them to bring in photographs and objects from home which they can talk about. There are many simple non-fiction books for children that will explain more about Hinduism and the festival of Divali.

Parents and carers as partners

At home, make some simple cold salt dough. Mix one cup of salt with three cups of flour, a teaspoon of oil (for stretchiness) and add a little water at a time to make dough. Add a drop of food colouring to change the colour. Keep it wrapped in cling film in the fridge. It can air dry slowly, but to keep it forever and make it hard enough to paint simply cook it in the oven on a medium heat until it is hardened. The dough can be used to make super decorations: roll it out like pastry and use cookie cutters to make shapes. Poke a paperclip into the top of your decoration before you cook it – it will set in the top and you can attach a hanging ribbon to it.

Autumn festivals and light

Activity 4

Rangoli patterns everywhere

The children will be making rangoli patterns from chalk, coloured rice or tessellated paper shapes and displaying them outdoors.

Resources

- ★ Pictorial examples of rangoli patterns
- ★ Coloured pegs and peg boards
- ★ Computer
- ★ ICT program such as PAINT
- ★ Coloured shapes
- ★ Squared paper
- ★ Chalks
- ★ Outside space with a hard surface

Storybooks and film clips

- ★ *Rangoli: Discovering the Art of Indian Decoration* by Anuradha Ananth
- ★ *Divali (Celebrations)* by Anita Ganeri

Observation and assessment

Expressive arts and design	Expected statements (ELGs)
Exploring and using media and materials	Children sing songs, make music and dance, and experiment with ways of changing them. They safely use and explore a variety of materials, tools and techniques, experimenting with colour, design, texture, form and function.
Being imaginative	Children use what they have learnt about media and materials in original ways, thinking about uses and purposes. They represent their own ideas, thoughts and feelings through design and technology, art, music, dance, role-play and stories.

Key vocabulary

- Goddess Lakshmi
- rangoli
- pattern
- shape
- rice
- chalk
- symmetry
- reflection
- decoration

What to do

Explain to the children that as part of Divali celebrations many Hindus choose to make decorations on the ground outside their homes, often on the doorstep. During Divali the Goddess Lakshmi is believed to visit homes that are well lit, so families decorate their homes and a rangoli pattern is created on the doorstep to welcome everybody. Show the children some examples of rangoli patterns and talk about the shapes and symmetry within them. They are usually geometric patterns formed with dots and lines, and can be very simple or incredibly complicated! Introduce the key vocabulary, and explain to the children that although the patterns are traditionally made with coloured rice they are going to use chalk, paper shapes, coloured pegs and the computer a PAINT program or similar (which has a symmetry line option) to make theirs.

Demonstrate creating the patterns in each of the different ways, talking through the colour and pattern choices made throughout. Ask questions of the children to see if they understand the idea of symmetry and pattern: Can they predict what colour pegs/which shape you will choose next? Why? Arrange a carousel of activities within the setting – four areas for rangoli pattern making, each with a different media. Provide some examples of simple patterns laminated for the children to take outside to copy in chalk. Explain to the children that they will be given the opportunity to create a pattern of each type. Whilst they are creating their patterns encourage the children to give reasons for their choices, and to consider colour, texture, shape and form.

If this is to be a guided activity...

...then the children can work together in a group with an adult to create a simple pattern on any of the four activities. The chalk must be suitable for use outdoors, and it may be necessary to pre-draw squares for the children to fill in with rangoli patterns, unless you have paving and a suitable area is evident. Otherwise you may find that the drawing stretches far and wide, and is not necessarily restricted to geometric patterns anymore!

If this is to be an independent activity...

...then explain to the children that over the forthcoming week they are to create up to four types of rangoli patterns: using ICT, chalk outdoors, pegboards and coloured shapes to tessellate. Their chosen method may have a paper outcome or can be stored on the computer, but if it is transient then provide the children with a digital camera so that they can photograph their work and it can be kept as evidence.

To support or extend

To support, let the children use the 2D flat shapes to make a pattern which is symmetrical. Monitor this with careful questioning and suggestion. If the child is unsure where the line of symmetry lies let them make their pattern on a tray and put a line of black sticky tape on the tray from top to bottom. Help them to place 2D shapes on either side of the line, choosing carefully considering colour, size and shape. As a follow up show them the computer program (e.g. PAINT) and set the page with a vertical line of symmetry. Let the children stamp shapes onto one side of the page on the screen and watch their delight and amazement when it is repeated 'as if by magic!' on the other.

To extend the more able children, encourage them to work independently to create a pattern first on squared paper before copying it onto a peg board. To extend further, use a whiteboard marker (as it will wipe off a smooth plastic surface) to draw one line of symmetry onto the board itself for the children to use when making a symmetrical pattern. Simply folding their squared paper will replicate the line of symmetry marked onto the peg board. Extend to two lines if they are capable. Allow the children to use mirrors to create symmetry on their boards, drawings and around the classroom.

Ideas for interactive display

Provide pegboards and crayons and squared paper to create simple rangoli patterns. Display photographs of actual rangoli patterns for the children to use as inspiration. The children can also make simple mendhi patterns by drawing around their hands on coloured paper and decorating the outlines with patterns, which are typically made with henna on skin.

Parents and carers as partners

At home, children can make simple patterns using household resources such as buttons, pasta, building blocks, clothes pegs or socks. To begin let the children make their pattern on a small surface like a placemat or a tray – but after that let them use the entire floor space!

Autumn celebrations

Celebrating autumn!

The final week of the topic is an opportunity to invite parents and carers into the setting to share some of the activities in which the children have been involved over the preceeding five weeks.

Tickell stated in her review that,

> *'Where parents and carers are actively encouraged to participate confidently in their children's learning and healthy development, the outcomes for children will be at their best'*

It is crucial that parents and carers are involved and feel able to support their children at every stage of development. This final week is, therefore, a time for the children to celebrate their successes, perform some of their new skills for their families to see and for parents and carers to be involved in their learning.

In the week building up to inviting the parents and carers into the setting the children can be involved in making invitations, decorations, food and practising songs, drama and dances to share on the special day.

The actual event can be really flexible in length, style and amount of parental involvement. Depending on the setting and the number of children involved it is possible to make this event an hour or a day long, or you may need to repeat it for two different cohorts of children. It could simply be an open style morning or afternoon for people to drop in, to look at things the children have made, or be a mini concert, where the children can perform dances, sing songs for the parents and afterwards share food the children have produced.

Whatever the design, the purpose is to share some of the activities and crafts the children have been involved in, and to celebrate the topic of autumn.

Listed opposite are ideas for celebration linked to each of the seven areas of learning, along with some ideas for parental involvement and understanding. The detailed expected ELG is also noted again here as a reminder of the expected level of attainment and understanding.

These are just some of the possible ideas – have fun, be creative and do whatever works for you and your children!

Ideas for an autumn festivals party

- Make invitations, cards and decorations – make invitations to the celebrations, hang strings of leaf outlines as bunting, make Divali cards and display rangoli patterns.

- Decorate the setting with some of the artwork produced – the colourful mixed leaves and onions, hang the 3D firework box models.

- Eat special food – make some bonfire toffee, firework biscuits, perhaps make some more hedgehog bread rolls and harvest vegetable soup to share with the parents and carers.

- Dress up in special clothing – allow the children to wear their best party clothes, autumn related fancy dress, or traditional Hindu clothing to celebrate Divali; decorate the children's hands with Mendhi patterns.

- Play party games – be an autumn animal when the music stops, dance like a bonfire flame or move like fireworks, listen to some traditional Hindu music and dance with scarves and floaty pieces of fabric.

Opportunities within Literacy

Aspect	Expected statements (ELGs)
Reading	Children read and understand simple sentences. They use phonic knowledge to decode regular words and read them aloud accurately. They also read some common irregular words. They demonstrate understanding when talking with others about what they have read.
Writing	Children use their phonic knowledge to write words in ways which match their spoken sounds. They also write some irregular common words. They write simple sentences which can be read by themselves and others. Some words are spelt correctly and others are phonetically plausible.

Most parents and carers are used to and comfortable with sharing books with children, as it is something that they have enjoyed regularly at home as their child has grown up. It is therefore a good idea to set up a corner within the setting with cushions, low tables and chairs to invite adults to sit quietly with the children reading, talking and listening. Put out a selection of books related to the topics, particularly including books that the children have seen before and which they have enjoyed in the setting. Include both fiction and non-fiction to appeal to a wide range of children and adults, and also include dual language texts. The children will relish being the expert when sharing the books with their parent or carer, and it gives a little quiet time to those finding the celebration a little busy.

Put out a writing area with a variety of suitable materials – include sticky labels, coloured sticky notes, postcards, envelopes, folded pieces of paper, lined, squared and dotted paper, old birthday or Christmas cards, old diaries and calendars and anything else the children would like to write upon! Include a mixture of pens, pencils and crayons. In this area also include blank invitations, Divali cards and autumn pictures to colour, cut and stick – the children and adults can have fun writing to each other and making cards or invitations. Children then see writing as having a purpose, and if there are a variety of materials which are easily found in a home setting it may give ideas to adults to encourage them to provide similar writing opportunities at home.

Opportunities within Mathematics

Aspect	Expected statements (ELGs)
Numbers	Children count reliably with numbers from 1 to 20, place them in order and say which number is one more or one less than a given number. Using quantities and objects, they add and subtract two single-digit numbers and count on or back to find the answer. They solve problems, including doubling, halving and sharing.
Space, shape and measures	Children use everyday language to talk about size, weight, capacity, position, distance, time and money to compare quantities and objects and to solve problems. They recognise, create and describe patterns. They explore characteristics of everyday objects and shapes and use mathematical language to describe them.

Let the children prepare for the adults visiting the setting by working out how many things will be needed for example: how many chairs altogether; how many around each table; how many cups or plates are needed? Setting the tables: have we enough; how many more; are they the same/equal? Extend this idea to the preparation of food when weighing for baking bread and biscuits, or measuring quantities for soup or bonfire toffee. These ideas are easily replicated at home, and the parents and carers can see how easy it is to provide simple mathematical activities at home without any special books or mathematical equipment.

Remind the children of the work they did on 2D shape (boat sails in the water tray) and 3D shape (box modelling fireworks). Put out shapes with the construction toys – can they use the different types of construction to make more boats and fireworks? Tell the children that they are to teach the adults how to do it. Ensure that there are clearly labelled pictures of the shapes and their names to encourage the visiting adults to use the correct vocabulary.

Opportunities within Understanding the world

Aspect	Expected statements (ELGs)
People and communities	Children talk about past and present events in their own lives and in the lives of family members. They know that other children don't always enjoy the same things, and are sensitive to this. They know about similarities and differences between themselves and others, and among families, communities and traditions.
The world	Children know about similarities and differences in relation to places, objects, materials and living things. They talk about the features of their own immediate environment and how environments might vary from one another. They make observations of animals and plants and explain why some things occur, and talk about changes.
Technology	Children recognise that a range of technology is used in places such as homes and schools. They select and use technology for particular purposes.

Make a display of the photographs that the children brought in of themselves and their families wearing different clothing. This will give an excellent starting point for the children to talk to their adults about a subject they know well – each other! Put the squirrel map work activity in the sand tray for the adults to play with their children. Most adults will understand how to play this and the children will enjoy challenging their parent or carer to a guessing game.

The use of ICT in the setting may be the most surprising to the parent and carer visitors. Ensure the computers and whiteboard are on (if you have them), digital cameras and voice recorders are available to use and toys such as programmable toys and pretend telephones and ovens are out for the children to show to the adults. Many parents and carers will believe that ICT relates only to computers: this is an opportunity to show them that technology includes the common objects in their own home.

A very simple but effective idea is to put all the photographs you have taken over the previous five weeks on as a slideshow – the children will love pointing themselves out, it is good evidence of the type of activities the children have been involved in and it will naturally prompt talk, listening and laughter.

Opportunities within Expressive arts and design

Aspect	Expected statements (ELGs)
Exploring and using media and materials	Children sing songs, make music and dance, and experiment with ways of changing them. They safely use and explore a variety of materials, tools and techniques, experimenting with colour, design, texture, form and function.
Being imaginative	Children use what they have learnt about media and materials in original ways, thinking about uses and purposes. They represent their own ideas, thoughts and feelings through design and technology, art, music, dance, role-play and stories.

Have an area set out as a place where adults and children can work together to produce decorations and artwork relevant to the topics looked at over the preceding five weeks. Provide paints for colour mixing to let the children show off their skills, or put the chalks outside for the children to replicate rangoli patterns on the floor. Providing simple pictures to complete and colour (e.g. autumn scenes, Divali lights or rangoli patterns) is also a popular activity which many adults recognise, and may choose to sit alongside children and participate in without any fear of 'doing it wrong'.

If your setting allows for it, prepare an area with some musical instruments and possibly a CD player with some traditional Hindu music. Let the children play the CD and investigate playing the instruments alongside. This activity works well outdoors, as there is more space for the children to dance and move with the instruments. The increased space may also enable children to feel 'free' and you may find that they initiate a marching band, making music and moving in time to it. If you extend their opportunities by also providing coloured scarves, fabric and masks they are also more likely to develop characters within the music and begin to role-play quite naturally. Parents and carers can see from this that expensive character fancy dress sets are not necessary – with only a couple of old hats and scarves they can provide valuable opportunities at home for dressing up and firing their children's imagination.

Opportunities within Communication and language

Aspect	Expected statements (ELGs)
Listening and attention	Children listen attentively in a range of situations. They listen to stories, accurately anticipating key events and respond to what they hear with relevant comments, questions or actions. They give their attention to what others say and respond appropriately, while engaged in another activity.
Understanding	Children follow instructions involving several ideas or actions. They answer 'how' and 'why' questions about their experiences and in response to stories or events.
Speaking	Children express themselves effectively, showing awareness of listeners' needs. They use past, present and future forms accurately when talking about events that have happened or are to happen in the future. They develop their own narratives and explanations by connecting ideas or events.

For some children who may usually find the setting a little overwhelming sharing their activities and successes with a familiar adult can be reassuring. They appreciate the time to be the expert, talking to their parent or carer about their daily activities and routines without the pressure to chat to a stranger or in front of others. For the practitioner in the setting this is also an ideal opportunity to listen quietly and unobtrusively to the child's conversation with others – it may be the first time you have heard the child speak!

Opportunities within Physical development

Aspect	Expected statements (ELGs)
Moving and handling	Children show good control and co-ordination in large and small movements. They move confidently in a range of ways, safely negotiating space. They handle equipment and tools effectively, including pencils for writing.
Health and self-care	Children know the importance for good health of physical exercise, and a healthy diet, and talk about ways to keep healthy and safe. They manage their own basic hygiene and personal needs successfully, including dressing and going to the toilet independently.

This area can link quite closely with Expressive art and design opposite where the children can move confidently and with control around the outdoor environment. It is useful for the parents and carers to note that young children need to have opportunities for physical play or movement several times a day, whether it is walking to school or running around the local park or garden.

There are many activities which encourage fine motor skills, including threading bead patterns; making rangoli patterns with coloured pegs and peg boards; building with construction or using pencils to trace, write, draw and colour. Parents can extend this at home very simply without any special equipment, for example by threading penne pasta onto string to make jewellery, using clothes pegs to hang out the washing; playing with small construction (e.g. Lego) or small world (e.g. a doll's house) or cutting pieces of baking paper for children to place over the pictures in their colouring book to use as a cheap alternative to tracing paper. It is vital that parents recognise these pre-writing skills as crucial in a child's fine motor development.

To promote good health and self-care it is useful to have a large display where the children (but more importantly, the parents and carers) can see it, showing which children can achieve such things as using the toilet independently, washing their hands, putting on their own coat or fastening their own shoes. Maybe have small photographs of each child, and when they have achieved the target then their photograph is moved onto, for example, a large outline of a coat. The children in the setting will then be very aware of what they need to do, and will take this information home in the form of pester power – quickly learning how to perform the skill! Sometimes parents and carers do not realise what is necessary for their child to become more independent.

Opportunities within Personal, social and emotional development

Aspect	Expected statements (ELGs)
Self-confidence and self-awareness	Children are confident to try new activities, and say why they like some activities more than others. They are confident to speak in a familiar group, will talk about their ideas, and will choose the resources they need for their chosen activities. They say when they do or don't need help.
Managing feelings and behaviour	Children talk about how they and others show feelings, talk about their own and others' behaviour, and its consequences, and know that some behaviour is unacceptable. They work as part of a group or class, and understand and follow the rules. They adjust their behaviour to different situations, and take changes of routine in their stride.
Making relationships	Children play co-operatively, taking turns with others. They take account of one another's ideas about how to organise their activity. They show sensitivity to others' needs and feelings, and form positive relationships with adults and other children.

Within the six week topic block there are continual opportunities for children to demonstrate their development in the aspect of PSED. Each activity throughout the previous weeks requires children to work together, co-operate, talk about their ideas, choose resources and form positive relationships with others. This final opportunity for celebration allows the children to show that this positive behaviour is embedded, as the key skill of 'adjusting their behaviour to different situations and taking changes in routine in their stride' is certainly tested during this busy week.

Make a note of any children who have struggled with certain aspects of PSED and ensure that they are prepared for this change in routine: pair them with a particular friend for security; provide them with a quiet space (e.g. a tent, a book corner, even another room in the setting with another group) to which they can escape when it becomes too much; give them a

key responsibility to prevent idle hands (such as handing out biscuits to adults, collecting empty cups or even tidying pencils and putting away chairs) or simply ensure that they are your 'special helper' and that they are to stay with you throughout the event. This way you are building on the personal, social and emotional capabilities of your children and allowing them to develop further within a safe and structured environment.

Ensure most importantly that parents and carers understand the uniqueness of each child. Measuring their child's attainment, progress and temperament against that of another child is of no benefit whatsoever. A child who feels loved, supported and a valuable member of their early years community will grow and develop into an adult that is able to love and support others, and more importantly will be a valuable member of any community they choose to belong to throughout the rest of their life.

Observation record: Characteristics of Effective Learning

Name: _____ DoB: _____

Characteristics	Date	Activity observed	Evidence (What did you see?)
Playing and Exploring • Finding out and exploring • Playing with what they know • Being willing to have a go'			
Through active learning • Being involved and concentrating • Keeping trying • Enjoying achieving what they set out to do			
By creating and thinking critically • Having their own ideas • Making links • Choosing ways to do things			

Group record sheet for Communication and language (**prime**) and Literacy (**specific**)

Date completed _____

Children's names	Communication and language (prime)									Literacy (specific)						
	Listening and attention			Understanding			Speaking			Reading			Writing		

Group record sheet for **prime** areas of learning (Personal, social and emotional development and Physical development)　　Date completed

Children's names	Personal, social and emotional development (prime)									Physical development (prime)					
	Self-confidence and self-awareness			Managing feelings and behaviour			Making relationships			Moving and handling			Health and self-care		

Group record sheet for **specific** area of learning (Mathematics)

Date completed _____

Children's names	Mathematics (specific)									Comments
	Numbers			Shape, space and measures						

Date completed

Children's names	People and communities	The world	Technology	Exploring and using media and materials	Being imaginative

Understanding the world (specific)

Expressive arts and design (specific)

Creative Planning in the EYFS © Lucy Peet

Planning overview: Autumn (weeks 1 - 2)

Week	Main topic and activities	ELGs covered from specific areas of learning			
		Literacy including some communication and language	Mathematics	Understanding the world	Expressive arts and design
1	**Autumn weather** • Autumn everywhere! • Windy sailing boats • Blowing along! • Wind whirlers and twirlers	Using their senses on an Autumn outdoor journey, and talking about it back in the classroom. Children express themselves effectively showing awareness of listeners' needs. They use past, present and future forms accurately when talking about events that have happened or are going to happen in the future. They demonstrate understanding when talking with others about what they have read.	Making sailing boats with 2D shaped sails to float animals in the water tray. Children count reliably with numbers from 1 to 20, place them in order and say which number is one more or one less than a given number. Children use everyday language to talk about size, weight, capacity, position, distance, time, and money to compare quantities and objects and to solve problems.	Using an electric fan to explore how different objects blow along. Children know about similarities and differences in relation to places, objects, materials and living things. Children recognise that a range of technology is used in places such as homes and schools. They select and use technology for particular purposes.	Choosing different materials to construct a ribbon stick to blow in the wind. Children sing songs, make music and dance, and experiment with ways of changing them. They safely use and explore a variety of materials, tools and techniques, experimenting with colour, design, texture, form and function. Children use what they have learnt about media and materials in original ways, thinking about uses and purposes. They represent their own ideas, thoughts and feelings through design and technology, art, music, dance, role-play and stories.
2	**Autumn animals** • Spiky poetry • Animal footprints • Nuts about nuts! • Handy hedgehogs	Extending their vocabulary by describing hedgehogs in a poem. Children listen attentively in a range of situations. They give their attention to what others say and respond appropriately, while engaged in another activity. They answer 'how' and 'why' questions about their experiences and in response to stories or events. They develop their own narratives and explanations by connecting ideas or events.	Using different animal footprints to count in groups. Children count reliably with numbers from 1 to 20, place them in order and say which number is one more or one less than a given number. Using quantities and objects, they add and subtract two single-digit numbers and count on or back to find the answer. They solve problems, including doubling, halving and sharing.	Making maps of squirrel nut hiding places and creating them in real life. Children know about similarities and differences in relation to places, objects, materials and living things. They talk about the features of their own immediate environment and how environments might vary from one another.	Printing handprints and cutting them out to make paper hedgehogs. They safely use and explore a variety of materials, tools and techniques, experimenting with colour, design, texture, form and function. Children use what they have learnt about media and materials in original ways, thinking about uses and purposes.

Planning overview: Autumn (weeks 3 - 4)

| | | ELGs covered from specific areas of learning | | | |
Week	Main topic and activities	Literacy including some communication and language	Mathematics	Understanding the world	Expressive arts and design
3	**Autumn food and harvest** • Exploring fruit and vegetables • Pumpkin soup • Hedgehog bread rolls! • Turnips and onions	Writing a 'Thank you for...' poem, listing favourite fruit and vegetables. Children use their phonic knowledge to write words in ways which match their spoken sounds. They also write some irregular common words. They write simple sentences which can be read by themselves and others. Some words are spelt correctly and others are phonetically plausible.	Following a recipe to make soup as an introduction to capacity. Children use everyday language to talk about size, weight, capacity, position, distance, time, and money to compare quantities and objects and to solve problems. They explore characteristics of everyday objects and shapes and use mathematical language to describe them.	Making bread in hedgehog bread roll shapes. Children know about similarities and differences in relation to places, objects, materials and living things. They make observations of animals and plants and explain why some things occur, and talk about changes. Children recognise that a range of technology is used in places such as homes and schools.	Mixing red and blue paint to make purple, and painting red onions looking at shades and tones. They safely use and explore a variety of materials, tools and techniques, experimenting with colour, design, texture, form and function. Children use what they have learnt about media and materials in original ways, thinking about uses and purposes.
4	**Autumn leaves and colours** • What's in the feely box? • Leaves on the line! • What shall we wear on a windy walk? • Patterned orange leaves	Describing natural Autumn objects to a partner after choosing them from a feely box. Children listen attentively in a range of situations. They give their attention to what others say and respond appropriately, while engaged in another activity. Children express themselves effectively, showing awareness of listeners' needs. They use past, present and future forms accurately when talking about events that have happened or are to happen in the future. They develop their own narratives and explanations by connecting ideas or events.	Leaf maths: ordering numbers on a line/ choosing different leaves to add to 6 Children count reliably with numbers from 1 to 20, place them in order and say which number is one more or one less than a given number. Using quantities and objects, they add and subtract two single-digit numbers and count on or back to find the answer. They solve problems, including doubling, halving and sharing.	Looking at photographs of themselves and their families at different times of year, looking at the weather and clothes worn. Children talk about past and present events in their own lives and the lives of family members. They know that other children don't always enjoy the same things and are sensitive to this. They know about similarities and differences between themselves and others, and among families, communities and traditions.	Mixing red and yellow paint to make orange and painting leaf outlines looking at shades, tones and pattern. They safely use and explore a variety of materials, tools and techniques, experimenting with colour, design, texture, form and function. Children use what they have learnt about media and materials in original ways, thinking about uses and purposes.

Planning overview: Autumn (weeks 5 - 6)

Week	Main topic and activities	ELGs covered from specific areas of learning			
		Literacy including some communication and language	Mathematics	Understanding the world	Expressive arts and design
5	**Autumn festivals and lights** • The story of Rama and Sita • Make 3D shaped fireworks • Lighting a lamp • Rangoli patterns everywhere!	Sharing the Divali story of Rama and Sita, and making masks in order to role play the story independently. They answer 'how' and 'why' questions about their experiences and in response to stories or events. They develop their own narratives and explanations by connecting ideas or events. Children read and understand simple sentences. They use phonic knowledge to decode regular words and read them aloud accurately. They demonstrate understanding when talking with others about what they have read.	Choosing appropriate 3D shapes to construct models of fireworks such as rockets. Children use everyday language to talk about size, weight, capacity, position, distance time and money to compare quantities and objects and to solve problems. They recognise, create and describe patterns. They explore characteristics of everyday objects and shapes and use mathematical language to describe them.	Making diva clay lights, understanding the significance and relevance to Hindus. They know about similarities and differences between themselves and others, and among families, communities and traditions.	Making rangoli patterns out of coloured rice or tessellated paper shapes. Children sing songs, make music and dance, and experiment with ways of changing them. They safely use and explore a variety of materials, tools and techniques, experimenting with colour, design, texture, form and function. Children use what they have learnt about media and materials in original ways, thinking about uses and purposes. They represent their own ideas, thoughts and feelings through design and technology, art, music, dance, role-play and stories.
6	**Autumn celebrations**			Ideas to share with parents and carers	